Simply Faithful
Finding the sacred in everyday life

Marketta Gregory

DEDICATION

These columns – and this book, really – happened almost by accident.

I was leaving the newspaper business for something with steadier work hours, something more suitable for my growing family. But as I turned to go, my editor at the *Rochester (NY) Democrat and Chronicle* asked if I'd keep writing, asked if I'd share my stories and opinions about faith and what people find sacred.

I was terrified, but I stumbled and started.

I'm so glad I did because in the last six years these newspaper columns have become a way for me to sort out what is happening in my heart and a way for me to capture my life with the people I love. If you read the pages of this book, you'll meet many of the people who mean the most to me, and you'll know this book is for them… and for you, dear friend.

When I started pulling the columns together I was shocked at how much I had shared about myself in 350-word bits, surprised at how well my readers might know me. But I pray my stories always point to the Greatest Story.

May you be blessed as you work your way through this book and may you know that God loves you more than you can imagine.

CONTENTS

EVERYDAY COLUMNS

Where church happens

For me, church is not just a building or even a group of people who worship and serve together – it's something that *happens*.

As a kid I went to a rustic church camp tucked away in the hills of Arkansas. When my youth group first started going there, the cabins didn't have air conditioning and you needed to wear rubber-soled flip flops in the shower to avoid a slight shock.

The centerpiece of the camp was the chapel and it had only a dirt floor and a tin roof. No walls. No frills. One night, it started to storm. Rain came down in sheets and slammed into the tin roof, making it almost impossible to hear anything else. Within minutes of the start of service water ran down the aisles and formed puddles among the uncomfortable pews.

But just when it seemed worthless to stay and try to listen, a man stood to sing the old Southern hymn "When the Roll is Called up Yonder." It was as if he had swallowed a microphone. His deep voice carried from the front of that soaked little chapel all the way to the back, and as the words from the song washed over the congregation, things began to change.

Teenagers started standing and thanking God for the changes they had seen in their lives, for the times he had helped them through rough spots and for the love he shared with them. Gratitude and grace entered the room and there, amid the mud and the rain, church happened –creating a moment that God might want to be part of, something sacred, powerful and unforgettable.

I've been back many times to that little chapel that now has a cement floor and a new roof. I've spent time in the opulence and beauty of the Vatican. I've had thoughtful conversations with groups of friends, and I've stood alone in my modest kitchen with just the buzzing of the refrigerator. In all of those places I've had extraordinary moments when I've felt close to God and faith has come alive for me.

Hopefully I'll have many more moments like that, wherever God would like to meet me.

Finding beauty in the chaos

They were there for me in the morning, the roses tipped with pink.

Not in the kitchen, where I get my morning water and greet the feisty Pomeranian. Not in the living room, where I sit to put on my shoes.

Instead, they sat on my desk in my office. The desk that was covered with books from the shelf that had to be moved for the cable guy. The desk that had a toddler's sweater draped over one corner and a globe cut in half waiting to be turned into lamp shades for the basement. The desk that barely had room for the vase.

I started to move them to a prettier area. Maybe the windowsill so I could see them in the natural light? The dining room table where nothing was piled and we could enjoy them as a family?

Instead, I left them there on the cluttered, things-almost-falling-off desk because I needed this reminder: I shouldn't look for beauty only in the parts that are already pretty. I should search for beauty in the middle of the mess.

I'm notorious for saying that I can't relax unless things are in order in the house – that I need at least one area that's calm and put together so I can feel better.

But maybe if I'm having trouble seeing the beauty, I should bring beauty with me to the chaos.

When dishes are stacked high and clean socks are hard to find, maybe I could bring patience and understanding.

That would be beautiful.

When things are falling apart and appointments are being missed, when tempers flare and feelings are hurt, maybe I could bring love and tenderness. And maybe I could bring them right to the uncomfortable spots where they are needed, right when they are needed most.

That would be really beautiful.

Maybe, like my husband, I could stop waiting on things to be perfect and push aside troubles and doubts (and all the things that clutter our minds) just long enough to change the whole landscape. Just long enough to make it beautiful.

When music works like a prayer

One of my favorite things growing up was listening to Mr. Tiger sing "Amazing Grace" at church.

Mr. Tiger didn't have a particularly strong voice or even much of a stage presence. In fact, he'd just go up to the front of our little wood-paneled church, stand between the pulpit and the congregation and start to sing in Creek, the language of his boyhood.

It wasn't often that I got to hear Creek or Cherokee or other Native American languages because for many of my classmates, those were the native tongues of their grandparents, of older aunts and uncles – languages that were at least one generation removed from us, even in a place once known as Indian Territory. So for me, hearing Mr. Tiger was a treat, a rare glimpse inside a wise and beautiful culture.

Eventually, of course, Mr. Tiger passed away, and I stopped looking for him at church. But I think of him often now that I'm 1,200 miles from where I grew up and am surrounded by people who don't talk like me and who might never have seen the sun set over a wheat field that seems to stretch from one end of the Earth to another.

I don't pretend to know what life was like for Mr. Tiger as he started to bridge the two cultures, one red and one white. But I do know that when he stood in front of us and sang in Creek it must have felt a lot like home to him. Sometimes he'd close his eyes, and I think the melody carried him back to times past like only music and language can.

I can never seem to adequately describe the power of music, but I know it preaches a good sermon all on its own and works like prayer to draw me closer to God and to remind me of sacred moments.

If I close my eyes, sometimes I can still hear the music of my childhood: the sound of a fiddle played late at night on a rickety front porch; the piano keys practically melting under my brother-in-law's fingers when he adds a little kick to old Southern hymns; my precious daddy singing loudly off-key. Suddenly, like Mr. Tiger, I'm home again.

Marking your blessings

I cry at the Hallmark channel and at the occasional country song, but even I was surprised when my eyes started to well up while checking Facebook the other day. A friend from long ago had posted a video made at her church, and it featured what they called cardboard testimonials.

It's a simple concept, really. You cut up a cardboard box and on one side you write a problem you faced. On the other side, you write how God helped you through it. In my friend's case, people took turns coming up to the front of the church. They showed their signs and then flipped them to show what God had done. One after another, after another.

- Breast cancer – survivor
- Used drugs to feel good – Use God to feel ecstatic
- Orphaned with no family – God provided a family
- Brother killed by drunk driver – I have forgiven
- $$$$ bondage – freedom obedience

For close to eight minutes the people stream by on the video, sharing some of the deepest parts of their souls in fewer than 10 words. I cried because of the pain they must have felt and I cried because I'm in love with hope, with overcoming the impossible.

And every time the cardboard signs turned over, there she was – hope scratched in black marker.

I'm sure many of us could hold up our own signs. I know I would have trouble deciding on just one:

- Will I ever be loved? – married April 18, 2003

- Drs said arm might not grow or move – played sports, trombone

I also have signs waiting for their happy endings, waiting for God to help me over, around – or even through – mountains of doubt and troubles. But those signs will come, too. Eventually I'll be able to flip them over and share testimonies of hope. My marker is ready.

The naming of a son

If everything goes according to plan, my third son will arrive shortly after 9:30 a.m. tomorrow. This time I'm not as afraid of giving birth, of figuring out the complicated car seat, of finding the right bumper for the crib. This time I'm more concerned about the intangible things I want for this son of mine.

I know it's popular to wish for happiness – for a life free of bumps and bruises – but I don't see that as practical or even helpful. Each generation has had its own challenges and its own evils: The good ol' days include slavery, the Holocaust and terrorist attacks that have killed thousands.

My son's generation will not be exempt from hardships either. And as much as I'd like to protect him, I'll serve him better by preparing him.

We're starting by giving him the first name Colt, which to me means strength and freedom. May he always have the courage to do the right thing, to look for God in every situation and to run to his side. May he always understand that freedom is a human right that comes from our Creator, not government – and may he be willing to stand for those rights, for himself and for others.

His middle name is Alexander, a name he shares with his oldest brother. On Friday, we'll celebrate three years of having that older brother live with us, an older brother who went through a tough time with his biological family and spent almost four years in foster care – an older brother who despite life's knocks has chosen compassion and progress. We could think of nothing better than those traits to have at the heart of a name.

May his middle name also serve as a reminder that true family is a choice, one we make every day in how we treat one another. May Colt never take family for granted and may he always feel loved and cherished.

May he find not only fleeting happiness but the deep joy that comes from finding a purpose in life, a life well spent in service to God and others. May he live up to – and beyond – his name.

Daddy was different in all the right ways

When it comes to daddies, I'd argue I had one of the best.

I have pictures of him pulling me as a toddler on a sled, of the two of us standing together the year he coached my softball team and side-by-side again at banquets, proms and graduations.

I have just as many pictures held not in my hands but in my heart: The portrait of him urging other church members to build a bigger building and promising to pay the mortgage himself if he needed to. The snapshot of him in front of his employees explaining that the company was downsizing but not to worry because he had found each of them jobs at nearby businesses.

And then, there's the uncomfortable picture of Daddy confronting our minister. It seems the minister didn't like a visitor who stopped by church, so he refused to shake hands with him. That didn't go over well with Daddy who believed God loves everyone.

At the peak of his career, the oil business in Oklahoma came to a near halt and other industries began to crumble. While others wringed their hands, Daddy was busy shaking hands with new opportunities. "Always be different, sis," he'd say. "Always be different."

The only thing that ever seemed to worry him was that something might happen to one of us three girls or to Mama. "They'd have to put me in the loony bin if I ever lost one of you," he'd say.

I think that's why he went first, before any of us. This week marks 10 years since his heart gave out on him, and for a while, it felt like my heart stopped beating, too.

That same minister who wouldn't shake hands preached at Daddy's funeral. When former employees were asked to be pallbearers, they said it would be an honor. Other people literally packed the hallway and spilled out into the parking lot. Cars lined up for more than a mile to escort Daddy to the cemetery.

Person after person told us what a difference Daddy had made in their lives, what joy and inspiration he had brought into every situation.

He was different, that daddy of mine. Different in all the right ways.

Decorating our homes and lives with scripture

I never met my great-granddad, but I know his fiddle. I grew up with it sitting on a shelf in our living room. Next to it always hung a picture that told how a master musician could take an old, discarded instrument and make beautiful music. It was a reference to how our broken lives become glorious in God's hands.

I saw that picture a million times, and I can still imagine it if I close my eyes because there's power in the things we see day after mundane day.

Mama and Daddy downsized and the large picture is long gone from the living room. But the last time we went home to Oklahoma we rented a little two-bedroom apartment that was filled with scriptures and quotes about faith.

For 10 days it seemed every room reminded us of God and his faithfulness.

And that's when the idea twirled by like those helicopters that fall from elm trees: Maybe the walls of my home needed to say more about God's goodness, more about his ability to turn brokenness into wholeness.

I began to search for scriptures that were beautiful in thought and in appearance, and I looked for sayings that offered real insight and value – like the one that hangs on the door to my home office, *Let us be silent that we may hear the whisper of God.*

I scoured our basement for a chalkboard and chalk, and I wrote in my best left-handed penmanship: *Pray without ceasing....* I propped it up on the empty eyesore that used to be our microwave stand and invited my husband and boys to list prayer requests.

Aunt Heather, who is pregnant, Jessie added.

Kathy's new job, I wrote. *Tanya's dad*, who is waiting on a liver transplant.

Benjamin wanted to pray for all the people who love him, and especially for his cousin JJ, whom he adores.

Next, I think I'll frame the words from my parents' picture and arrange it on my mantel in the living room. I'll put it right next to my great-granddad's old fiddle, which I inherited. And when it's time to pass the beloved fiddle on to the next generation, I'll make sure my boys have the words, too.

God is enough

We all know that life is full of highs and lows, of gleeful rides to the top of the Ferris wheel followed by the slow and rocky descent to the ground. That's where I found myself last week – in the slow and rocky part.

I was spent. I was tired from working outside the home and exhausted from dealing with family budgets and laundry and Legos. It seemed everyone, from my boss to the family Pomeranian needed something from me. Colt, who is usually a Daddy's boy, cried every time I left the room. Benjamin begged me to play with his super hero guys, read a third story and make another treasure map. Jessie needed help with a Valentine's Day card, and Brian and I were arguing over every little thing.

Everyone felt neglected, and no one was getting what he wanted.

"I can't please anyone," I half mumbled, half prayed. "I can't make anyone happy. There's just not enough of me."

There is plenty of me, a quiet, loving voice told me. *I am enough.*

I hadn't really been expecting guidance. I only wanted a listener, and even as I let those words hang there, in my heart I wanted to complain more, to argue and make my case that too much was being asked of me. But I couldn't.

If I claim to believe in an all-powerful God, then don't I have to believe he is all powerful?

It's so simple, yet I need to be reminded to live that concept out – reminded to trust that, even on the slow and rocky parts, I'm not on the Ferris wheel alone.

How to deal with frogs and apologies

I don't know if it's the closeness of the Arkansas River or a perfect mix of vegetation, but for some reason frogs always gathered in my parents' driveway. Every evening, about the time the floodlight kicked on, we'd hear them by the garage. Big ones with bellies that barely cleared the grass when they hopped. Tiny ones that jumped from rock to rock on the gravel.

So, it was no surprise that the night my boyfriend came to meet my parents a few frogs were there to greet us. Even though we were both in our 20s, he was nervous – that is until he saw the frogs. "Can I catch one?" he asked, smiling like he was 8. "Sure," I said, "But watch out. They'll pee on you."

I don't think I had finished the sentence before he started chasing the frog that looked like the teenager of the family. Charlie would take a step toward it and the frog would jump out of his way. "You've got to get beside it so you can put a hand in front," I advised.

A few seconds later, Charlie had his frog. He gingerly held it in his hands and then cradled it to his chest so he could get a better look at it. And that's when it happened. Pee soaked his hands and the front of his meet-the-father shirt.

We had no choice but to go inside. When my dad rose to greet him, he offered his hand to Charlie, who apologized and said he'd need to wash up first. When he returned from the restroom, he sat in my parents' living room and laughed and talked like nothing had happened.

For reasons that had nothing to do with frogs, our relationship didn't last long. Still, I've come to respect how he handled the situation. Too often I try to be perfect and poised. I beat myself up for not keeping my New Year's resolutions, for the stack of laundry in the basement and for hundreds of other ways I don't have my life together.

Maybe it's time I, too, said a quick apology, washed my hands and moved on. Maybe it's time I accepted a little grace. And I could just throw that dirty shirt in with the rest.

Getting to church

It's true that pride comes before a fall because I was pretty smug about having my entire family take showers on Saturday night and pick out their church clothes for the next morning. This was going to be the week, the week that we got to church on time.

Usually my goal is arriving before the nice, organized family with 10 kids, but I'd been dreaming of going beyond that, of actually being seated before the songs started. So, I was taking action, that is until our 2-year-old yelled, "No pants! No pants!"

"You absolutely have to wear pants to church," I explained as I wrestled to slip the right leg on before he kicked off the left. Then, our 10-year-old walked into the room wearing a striped polo that was on backward and baggy camouflage pants that I'm pretty sure he had played in for two days.

"Is this OK?" he asked. I suggested different pants, perhaps solid-colored ones, but I did not say a word about the fact that his shirt was facing the wrong direction. And when he came back wearing slacks with one leg tucked into a white tube sock, I still said nothing. Time was slipping away from me – and so was his bare-bottomed little brother.

Somehow my husband and I dressed, let the fluffy dog out and got the boys in the car, only to discover we didn't have diapers with us and that we hadn't fed our family. Fifteen minutes and one fast-food stop later, we arrived at church. Late.

Our oldest son, who had switched his shirt around by this time, headed to children's church, but the youngest screamed when we got within five feet of the nursery. The three of us settled into a pew near the back just in time for a prayer and just in time for the little guy to say, "Mommy poopa pants." Loudly. More than once. I was never so glad to hear an amen.

Maybe it was grace, but the rest of the service went smoothly, and we laughed all the way to the car. "Jesus cool," we heard from the toddler in the car seat.

Success, after all.

Serving with Parkinson's

Sometimes people ask me to tell them about my most interesting interviews. They get really quiet, expecting to hear me rattle off a list of famous names that I've scratched down in my skinny reporter's notebook.

But the people who come to my mind first are the ones whose names you probably wouldn't recognize. There's the boy in Oklahoma who donated bone marrow to save his little brother's life. If I remember correctly, he was about 9 when he became one of my heroes. And there's the woman here in Rochester who walks the streets helping prostitutes and the homeless get the medication they need as they battle AIDS and other diseases. What others turn away from, she looks squarely in the eyes.

Then, there's the late Rev. Elmer Schmidt. When I met him five years ago, he was living at the Sisters of Mercy Motherhouse in Brighton. He had most recently served at St. Anne Church in Rochester. That is, until the Parkinson's stole so much of his health.

By the time I met him, the disease had taken most of his voice. He spoke only in whispers -- between long breaks for breath -- as he told about his stiff and stubborn hands and his crumbling legs. His thoughts were still there, but it was hard to concentrate, he said, and hard to bring them out in to the open.

I got the impression that he normally wouldn't have talked so much about his illness, except that I had asked. You see, at the time, Pope John Paul II was suffering from the same disease and there were some who thought the pope should step aside. I was there to shake hands with the disease, so to speak, to be close enough to describe it to my readers. But what I shook hands with that day was life -- a life altered, to be sure, but a life still adding others to its prayer list.

"It helps you to feel wanted, needed," he told me that day, still ministering from his wheelchair. "You have to feel needed or you fold up."

I often think of him, there in his simple room willing his facial muscles to let him smile. I never knew him at what others might consider his best, but I'd argue that I met a man that day determined to serve God and others regardless of his circumstances.

When I pray for God to wrap his arms around those who are suffering, sometimes my mind drifts back to that interview. And I ask God to slip plenty of joy in with the comfort. Amen.

Trusting the Author

Grandma Gregory could spin a tale like nobody's business. She'd take a routine trip to the corner store and turn it into the kind of story that you'd asked her to tell again and again.

And when she started in on the stories about how tiny Daddy was as a baby, you could practically see the dresser drawer he slept in and the little doll clothes he wore.

So, you can imagine the kinds of letters she wrote to her children. One of my favorites is her party invitation to fill in a ditch. She promises games for the children and wheelbarrow and shovel racing for the adults.

In another letter, postmarked March 25, 1978, she wishes my parents a happy Easter. In it, she writes about how she cherishes her memories from the Easter of 1977 – the year the two of them dedicated their lives to serving God and were baptized. That Easter season, Grandma's "dream of a lifetime" came true, she writes, before she goes on to encourage them:

"… we'll come in contact with many things we don't understand but read your Bible, keep your eyes on Jesus and your hand in his and he will take you through to the end."

She wrote all of those things before sickness took her husband and diabetes took her legs, before terrorists slammed airplanes into the World Trade Center, before tsunamis raked away entire towns and villages and radiation threatened to poison the survivors.

Now, all these years later, I still find comfort and wisdom in her long-ago letter.

She reminds me to pray not only for protection, but for strength.

Grandma spent most of her life trying to crawl into God's arms and trying to share his love with others. She was OK with not understanding everything, OK with not knowing how every story ended.

She simply trusted the author.

Knowing God's heartbeat

I found out by accident that my first son knew my heartbeat. He started to cry a few hours after he was born, and I picked him up and happened to rest his head near my heart. Within seconds Benjamin calmed down and was comforted by the familiar thump, thump, thump.

It didn't work when my husband held him next to his heart. Benjamin could hear and smell the difference, and it was me he wanted.

With Colt, it's my voice that soothes. When he's upset, I put my mouth near his ear and whisper that I'm there, that everything's OK. My cheek brushes against his. He reaches out to hold my finger and he quiets. The redness in his face fades to pink. I'm the one he's most used to, the one who offers the most security and peace.

And I like that.

When I first became a mom, I knew I'd spend the first few weeks memorizing the boys' faces. I'd learn the meaning of their cries, and I'd cherish the first time they each raised their chubby arms to hug my neck. But I didn't realize that they already knew so much more about me and the body we had shared.

In the moments after birth, they didn't need an introduction. They knew where they had come from and where they belonged.

I want to be that way with God. I want to know him so well that I never have to question if he's on my side because I'll already be standing next to him. I want to be close enough to his face that I can hear him when he whispers – and I want to listen and take action before there's a need for him to raise his voice or to get my attention in other ways.

I want to know him so well that I barely have to question if something is in his will or if he is who he says he is. I want to be where I belong, curled up next to his heart listening to the thump, thump, thump and knowing that, like Benjamin and Colt, I'm safe and loved.

The hiccups of faith

It's not the big theological questions that bug me. It's the hiccups: The irritating things that I didn't expect or plan for. The things that interrupt what I'm trying to do or say. The things that start out small, but over time, become all I can think about.

I'm a planner by nature, or, more accurately, a controller. I've been known to create five-year plans for both my career and my personal life. And I've been known to get the hiccups.

I've seen it in other people's lives, too. Relatives who have lost a couple of jobs and are now struggling to sell their house in a down market — a home they planned to make a profit on for retirement. Friends who have had to close their once profitable businesses. Others who gave their marriages everything they had, only to watch their spouses walk away.

Life. Interrupted. Unplanned for.

That messiness grates on my faith. I'm not swayed by the debate over once-saved, always-saved or opinions on end-time prophecies. But I struggle with the unexpected and the disappointments.

Deep down, I think good people shouldn't have to suffer, and if you work hard, you should always be rewarded with a job. And I get a little upset at God when life doesn't turn out that way, when the hiccups turn painful.

I know he sees the top of a beautiful tapestry when all I can see are the knots on the underside. I get that on an intellectual level. It's heart-level where the trouble comes in. My expectations slink up behind me and whisper in my ear that God is distant, uninterested. Hiccup.

But usually, just as I start to complain, I remember times when God soothed my hiccups — when, like a long, cold drink of water, he made them more bearable. And, now looking back, I can see what I learned from those interruptions and inconveniences. I know, even at heart-level, that I'm stronger because of them.

So, I pray for those who are going through the hiccups now, and I hold my breath until they go away.

Sandpaper on the soul

It was a calm weekend, one where the kitchen was clean and the sewing machine was out on the craft table. I had shooed the two older boys out to the backyard, and I was listening through the open window as they argued and played, argued and played.

My goal was to create quiet books, the kind where you sew a bit of a plastic page protector to cardstock and essentially create a write-on, wipe-off board. The first seam went well, but just as I started the second, the thread slipped out of the needle leaving empty punctures where I had envisioned a zigzag stitch.

Since I was working with cardstock and not fabric, those holes were as noticeable as potholes on an otherwise smooth street. Where I had wanted perfection, I now had an ugly snag. And the only way to bind the slick page protector to the cardstock was to rethread the needle and make more punctures. I knew glue wouldn't hold for long, especially with such a slippery surface.

I thought of books and newsletters, of staples and lasting binding. All holes. All punctures. I thought of paint slapped on polished wood, ready to chip almost as soon as it dried. And paint applied to a rough surface, forever in the cracks and crevices of a concrete overpass. It seems nothing binds for long when perfect and smooth, when only surface level is applied to only surface level.

I like surface level, where everything looks glossy and everyone gets along. I'd rather skip talking about my spiritual shortcomings and my irritating habit of leaving shoes in a pile by the door. But that's a slippery way to bind a relationship that you want to keep, one that will hold tight when troubles and time tug.

God seems to have no problem poking holes in my struggles. My faltering patience gets sewn in with a panel of grace. When the needle strikes next, it's my nagging self doubt that's forever pulled tight to touch the fabric of his greatness.

The puncturing always comes first, though, before the healing. It's uncomfortable at times, and unpleasant. No one likes the feeling of needle pricks or of sandpaper on the soul, but it's necessary to scratch at the smooth surface, to dig a little deeper. There's just no other way to bind hearts.

Finding the right Jesus

About a year ago I dipped my toes into the virtual waters of Facebook. I'll admit, it was purely due to peer pressure. Everyone was talking about it, and I was feeling left out of the water cooler chatter.

So, one weekend I stole some time away and crept upstairs to our home office. In a matter of minutes I created a simple page, found a recent picture of myself and started looking for people to link up with, people who would accept my "friend" request. I found a good friend from high school who I had lost contact with, my nephew who lives in another state and plenty of my church friends, whose family pictures I now get to see on a regular basis.

Then, the idea hit: I wanted to be friends with Jesus Christ.

Really, how cool would that be? He could update me on what he's doing, make comments on the cute pictures I post of my kids, offer some credibility to my page and maybe even play me in an on-line game of Scrabble – although somehow I think he'd win.

But with so many Jesus Christs on Facebook, how would I choose the one I wanted to be associated with?

I could go with the Jesus Christ who had the most fans, but it didn't seem right to make a weighty decision like this based solely on numbers. I glanced through the profile pictures and eliminated the ones that didn't fit my image of Jesus, and then I started to narrow by beliefs.

I was shopping for a Jesus who was true to the Bible, who was loving and who would have my back if I got in trouble. I didn't mind if he was a little controversial, but I didn't want him to go overboard. He needed to agree with my political ideas and, well, the list went on and on until I started to feel uneasy, unqualified to put my own parameters on Jesus. I clicked off Facebook.

The whole idea seemed a lot less funny than it had at first. And a little too real.

The marathon of life

It's not often that I knowingly cross paths with people who have run multiple marathons. I'm not a runner myself, or even an occasional jogger, so it was just by chance that I was introduced recently to a man who had run 19 marathons.

I've always figured that casual runners respected the endurance of those who run marathons the same way I look up to gifted poets. And I figured that anyone passionate enough to complete multiple marathons would be the kind of person who insisted on keeping in shape, always training for the next big race. But this man wasn't. In fact, when I met him, he was talking about the need to begin training again and while he talked, he patted his stomach.

It would take a little while, he said, to get going again. Odd, I thought. With all those races and all that experience behind him, he would still have to start at the beginning. He would still need to prepare.

Unfortunately, I think I'm in the same place spiritually. I've been doing my best to serve God for many years. In fact, by some people's standards, I'm even considered experienced because I've run some faithful races. I've relied on God for some heavy stuff. Like being the first in my family to navigate going to college. Like moving by myself across the country. Like enduring painful loss.

All that praying and scripture reading I did years ago, when I was really training, carried me through those early races. But now I'm in the marathon of marriage and motherhood, of trying to become a mature woman of God – and I feel just like my new friend, the runner. I need a little while to get going again, a little time to prepare and build my endurance.

It's time for me to stop taking short cuts and commit to doing the work I know I need to do. I know the things that feed my soul.

Knowing who you are

With a name like Marketta, you're bound to have nicknames. That is, unless you have a mama like mine.

Growing up there were countless people who tried to shorten my name but each person was corrected – firmly – by Mama. She named me Marketta, she'd say, and that's exactly what she wanted me to be called.

At times it was a little frustrating, and even a tad embarrassing when I was a teenager, but on this one point Mama was unmovable. I had no choice but to go along with it.

Somewhere along the way, I guess I succumbed to the brainwashing because I started to get irritated when people said my name was too difficult to pronounce or when they'd ask if I had a nickname that was easier to remember.

"You can call me Marketta," I'd hear myself say firmly. And then I started to get it, how this really wasn't a battle over nicknames. I got a glimpse of what Mama had been trying to teach me: Not to budge on who I am.

Life has a way of knocking us down and trying to slap labels on our foreheads. If we listen to some people, we can start to believe we're failures or we're lazy – that we're not contributing anything of meaning and that we're not worth remembering, no matter how short our names are.

It's one of the biggest lies in the universe, this idea that we're defined by what naysayers think of us or by what they want to call us. Still, sometimes I fall for it. That is, until I remember who I am and whom I serve.

I believe in a God who literally filled the depths of the oceans and placed each star precisely in the sky, a God whose power and compassion I can't even begin to describe. And in my mind, it's that awe-inspiring God who says we're loved, forgiven and cherished. I can't help but give his opinion a little more weight than what the average person thinks.

He says we're worth remembering. In fact, we're worth it all.

He even says it firmly. And I believe him.

The importance of a peaceful dwelling

Of the three of us sisters, I've always been the least domestic. Kathy is the organizer, the cleaner and the baker of buttermilk cakes. Jaquita is the one who decorates, plans parties and makes the dressing at Thanksgiving, and I... well, I'd like to use my kitchen cabinets as bookshelves.

Now that I have a family of my own – one husband, three boys and an aging Pomeranian – I really am trying to keep clutter at bay and the floors mopped because I want a welcoming and restful home.

Still, you'd think I would have taken care of the scratches we put on the wall when we crammed an overstuffed sectional down the stairs to the basement. Or hung up those beautiful pictures of the boys that we had printed in July. Or carried my shoes upstairs to my closet. Or. Or. Or.

For years I've felt guilty because my home is not as pristine as I'd like, but it's finally starting to sink in that God doesn't ask for perfect houses. He just wants us to have peaceful homes where we rest in his love.

I'm trying to do just that by not lecturing about homework and grades at the dinner table or right before bed, by hugging more and reaching out to hold a hand – even while we're arguing. By turning off the TV and letting the iPad sit idle while we bend pipe cleaners into the shapes of hearts, candy canes and slightly lopsided circles. By modeling forgiveness and grace. By deciding that when God talks about loving my neighbor, he also means the neighbors who live in my house.

Oh, I still fail. I get stressed out. I bark at the kids. I interrupt the 5-year-old's long story about the city he'll build one day and the hotel we'll all live in. I linger too long on the mistakes and the negative because it's a lot of work, this loving business.

A perfect home is something you can hire someone to create for you. A peaceful home is something you have to live out yourself.

It can get messy and difficult, but it's worth it. I'm sure of it.

The hash mark of April 19

Some events in life are so substantial that they leave a big hash mark on our personal timelines. They make it clear that there was a time "before" and a time "after."

For most of us, those events are things like a high school graduation, marriage, the birth of child – or a tragedy, like the death of someone dear to us or an unimaginable event like the bombing of the Alfred P. Murrah Building in Oklahoma City.

If you could see my timeline, the bombing hash mark would be in bold, a clear division between feeling secure and understanding that terrible things really can happen, even to good people.

Who would have imagined that Oklahoma would be a target for terrorism? My home state isn't huge or heavily populated, unless you count the cattle. We don't have enough electoral votes to bother anyone. And we're pretty well mannered. We still hold the door open for each other and pull over to the side of the road when a funeral procession passes to show our respect.

But 15 years ago today, we learned that we, too, are vulnerable. At 9:01 a.m., life was normal. By 9:03 a.m., my world had forever changed.

Since then, I've seen the Twin Towers fall. I've watched earthquakes shake entire countries, and I've witnessed a powerful tsunami, miners pulled from rubble and students running from gunmen.

Sometimes I'd like to rub my eyes and start over – go back to the time before my April 19th hash mark. But then I remember the strength and the goodness I have seen in others who have chosen to be brave and compassionate in the most difficult of times.

Rescue workers flooded Oklahoma and worked around the clock, giving us all they possibly could. Restaurants delivered free food to the site. Families and college students scoured their closets for raincoats, blankets and flashlights – and anything else the rescuers needed.

And I'll never forget the First United Methodist Church, which sits next door to the Murrah property. The church, which had been used as a makeshift morgue in the hours after the bombing, hung signs where its beautiful stained glass windows had once been: "Our God reigns & we will remain."

Vulnerable, yes. Defeated, no.

On the porch with Mama

When Mama comes to visit, we are assured of two things: There will be chocolate gravy for breakfast and there will be time on the porch.

The older she gets and the more her legs ache? The more we sit.

It's always hard at first, this sitting – this slowing down of mind and spirit. It's not that I'm used to doing or moving too much. It's that I'm used to worrying that I do too little. My thoughts love to wander into areas that are spotted with "I should…" and "Don't forget to…"

No matter how fast I work, I can't out run my mind.

Still, I want time with Mama so I sit. I listen to Mama tell me how they are searching for a new preacher in our home church, how she isn't sure she'll be able to keep the family history book up-to-date now that Aunt Louise is gone. I tell her Colt's speech therapy is going well and Benjamin loves his art class, that Jessie prayed for a kid who has been bullying him.

We add another cup of bird seed to the feeders and call the boys out to see the cardinals and the robins and the smarty pants squirrel who hangs upside down to scrape out a snack. We bring out more chairs and make tea.

By the middle of her trip, I'm reading to the boys by the dim shine of the patio lights. And when they can't find me at the computer, or in the kitchen or down in the basement doing laundry, they know to look on the porch – where there is important work, too.

Work toward being content, not only with what I have but with what I've gotten done. Work toward understanding that I might be able to simplify my life just by simply letting go of some of my own expectations. Work toward knowing that this needs to last after Mama goes home and I return to my normal routine. Work toward grasping that I need more than a vacation. I need a sabbath.

I need the sacred gift of rest, not just from tangible tasks that pile high but from the work orders my mind barks out. The "I shoulds" are always clamoring for attention. They'll take as much as they can get, especially when there are no limits, no hard stops.

Sabbath interrupts the habit. It stops the running. It retrains the mind and nourishes the soul.

And it teaches me that the more I ache from busyness and stress, the more I need to sit.

Building tree houses – and joy

If you've ever driven to School of the Holy Childhood in Henrietta, NY, chances are you've passed by the yard of Maurice and Marie Barkley. And if you're observant – at all – you've noticed a large village of tree houses perched high above the Barkleys' corner lot.

As the story goes, the Barkleys' grandchildren wanted a platform built in a tree at Grandpa and Grandma's house. Maurice built it, and by the time the grandchildren asked for a bridge, Grandpa was hooked. Now, he adds on one fanciful structure each year and welcomes young and old to explore the high-in-the-sky kingdom – and the idea that one can build for pleasure, not merely for calculated resale value.

If I were Marie Barkley, I would have been skeptical of my husband's imaginative project. I would have worried about what the finished project would look like and questioned whether the expense and the upkeep would be worth it. I might have even worried about all those sightseers trampling my irises or sneaking into my yard when I wasn't home. You see, unlike Marie, I would have come dangerously close to missing the gift that Maurice's labor of love offers: Pure joy.

I know I'm not alone, especially in this country where sometimes people don't slow down enough to take all of the vacation days that they've earned. We seem to always want something valuable to show for our time. We want to work toward finishing society-approved projects, like remodeling our kitchens or detail cleaning our new cars. We can rarely be bothered with risky things like an unscheduled day to enjoy our families and friends or a project that results only in beauty or fun. No, those things can come later, after we've finished our work.

But the Barkleys have made a different choice. They drink coffee high up in the trees each spring and watch as God thoughtfully dips each leaf in gold and red in the fall. They welcome neighbors and newly made friends alike to explore their tree church, tree houses and other tree buildings. And those brightly colored, well maintained structures remind us to dream a little and to share what brings real joy to our souls. Quite a lesson for us all.

Paying attention to the right thing

I wasn't surprised when I walked into the model train room and saw Jessie leaning over a track while two gentlemen with gray hair pointed to train cars. It's hard not to get into a conversation with the volunteers at the New York Museum of Transportation. It's a small place run on donations, the love of trains and the joy of tinkering.

These volunteers are the kind who strap tiny cameras to engines and hook up a feed to a nearby TV so kids can see what it's like to round the curves and pass the miniature Ferris wheel. They are the kind of handy men who start to tell a boy how to fix his train and wind up working with him and repairing it on the spot.

So, when I walked by Jessie I nudged him and jokingly asked if he had broken something. *No, just helping get this back on the track*, he said, laughing and lingering by the table.

The two younger boys and I went on to watch the model trains chug through a tunnel and then we moved on to drive an antique fire truck and pretend to serve passengers in the dining car. Jessie stayed behind, still tinkering until it was time to leave.

That night, over dinner, I asked Jessie, *Did you ask to see something or did the gentlemen just offer to show you what they were working on?*

One of the men was trying to get the train back on the track. I noticed his hand was shaking, Jessie said, *so I asked if I could help him. That particular track is a little tricky. You have to get the cars just right.*

And there it was. My son who fidgets. My son who usually rushes past details.

That son.

He noticed the most important detail of all.

Matryoshkas and making room for God

I suspect even the most dedicated collector has favorites. That one quartz he found on vacation as a boy. The postage stamp that came on the first letter from her pen pal. At least it's true for me, a recovering doll collector. Of all the dolls in my collection, there are a few that are always top of mind.

There's the one in the tattered yellow dress. Nancy is her name. She was the one Mom bought me when I was a baby. The one I most liked to play with.

Then, there's the Madame Alexander doll my best friend's mom gave me – Cinderella with a shiny blue dress. It had been hers growing up and she wanted me to have it because she knew I'd treasure it. She was right.

But the dolls I always have on display at my house are my matryoshkas. I love the artistry of each nesting doll, and I like the visual reminder that we all have layers of stories to tell just beneath the outer surface.

A few of my Russian nesting dolls show women in intricately painted aprons, and two display Russian cities with shining domes. But my favorite set of dolls shows a series of religious icons, starting with Mary and baby Jesus. Four other icons are inside and sometimes I open up the set and display them all.

The last time I opened them and rearranged them, I paused when I got to the one that showed Jesus as an adult. I admired the gilded halo and the soft eyes, but just as I started to set it down, I noticed the empty shell of the larger doll.

To make room for Jesus, the first shell had to be emptied. The wood had to be carved and shaped and then, ever so carefully, crafted to fit back together.

Is it really so different for us?

For faith to have a place within, something else has to be carved out. Greed and gossip must go because love and humility and sacredness need space to grow.

It's not an easy process, this letting go of selfishness to make room for what makes our selves better. But it does no good to paint the outside without clearing out the inside because without the clearing, the story ends before its time.

Instead of five nesting dolls, the story stops at four. Or at three.

The beauty that the artist had hoped to share is stunted. The story is shallow and the masterpiece unfinished.

So, we can hold on and remain intact, or we can let go and be made whole.

Reflecting love

We were in the middle of a bible study, all comfortable in our chairs, when the conversation turned to light and to God's love.

Our lives should be a reflection of that, someone said. *We should show his love to the world.* We all nodded and discussed the next verse. But after the closing prayer and the homemade toffee and the catching up with friends, after the drive home, I wondered about that word reflection. And I started to unpack its meaning.

I thought of seeing my face in mirrors and in clear, calm waters – and how the slightest wind or bend would cause distortion. I thought of how light reflects off of but rarely in to, how it deflects rather than absorbs. And I thought of how, without the source of light being visible, the reflection quickly grows dark or non-existent.

While my friend meant reflection as something to aspire to, I began to see it as an unfortunate description of where I sometimes am. I know I share God's love best when life is peaceful and there are no ripples in the pond. And I struggle when the really hard times come, when evil scratches hard all around. I strain to position myself to see the light, and I forget that the light is already in me.

But when I think of God's love as something within, then it becomes a light that can stand alone in the darkness, a light that shines brightly in spite of circumstances. It becomes something I bring with me when I stand with the mourning and when I welcome the stranger. It becomes something sustaining, purifying and transformative.

It becomes what I believe it was meant to be.

Stretching to serve

Colt is at the age where he can reach new things every day. The door handle that was too far of a stretch yesterday is turning in his little palm today, and that cup we left on the counter, well, now it's on the floor.

This time, thankfully, it was only a damp washcloth that he grabbed. I carried it out to give the table its final cleaning for the day and just turned my back for an instant to hush the little dog.

Colt already had it that quickly. He had to stand on his toes, but he was wiping the very edge of the table. I scooped him up and let him stand on a chair, and he continued to clean. When he reached a tiny piece of leftover cheese, he carefully picked it up and handed it to me. I applauded. Then, he called for "Da" to come see what a big boy he was.

While Dad hovered by the chair, I went to get the camera. Our littlest guy was doing what he could to help, and I was proud of him. By the time I'd made it to the closet and was unbuckling the camera bag, my smile had faded a bit – not because I was any less pleased with Colt, but because I was embarrassed before God.

How long had it been since I stretched myself all the way to my toes to do something for him? When was the last time I took on a task without first worrying how it would turn out, without wondering how it would measure up to other people's standards?

Colt didn't mind the work at all, even though it was difficult for him. He just so badly wants to be like us that he'll imitate almost anything. And if we smile or clap, he'll do it over and over and over.

How badly do I want to please God? How badly do I want to mold my life in his ways?

By the time I made it back down the hallway and snapped a few pictures of Colt, my heart was plotting ways to change, ways to reach both farther and further.

A picture of prayer

We planned our entire trip around my sister's party, the one where the sky above her Oklahoma neighborhood explodes with color after color. The party where I knew my boys could light smoke bombs and watch their cousins set off rockets, where we could drink from red, white and blue straws and laugh until our bellies hurt.

My boys aren't used to firework stands dotting the roadways from June to July. They are growing up in an area that's more heavily populated and more heavily regulated. And just this once, I wanted them to light a fuse, see it flicker and run like crazy to the sidewalk.

I wanted this little sliver of Americana for them. The Fourth of July the way I remembered it growing up.

I probably took 200 pictures that night. My husband with his first ever firework. Colt throwing tiny sacks that pop when they hit the ground. Benjamin holding sparklers with the sun setting in the background. Jessie chasing a wayward parachute.

Then, there's the picture of Colt and Aunt Kathy holding a tiny frog and the photo of the cousins in their matching flag shirts. A snapshot for every moment I wanted to capture and savor.

When the noisy firecrackers were gone and the smoke had dissipated, when I was just about to put away the camera for the night, we brought out the paper lanterns and began to unfold them.

There in the relative quiet, we separated the walls of the lanterns and made room for the flame and the hot air that would follow. Each lantern had a person on each side, waiting for the globe to lift. Then, ever so slightly, the lantern pressed against their hands and slowly and reverently rose.

I have no idea how long we stood there watching, pointing to our distant lights, but I know I've thought of it often since then – thought of it as a visual prayer.

In the chaos and the darkness, with firework casing all around, we opened up the walls to make room for God. We were still and we waited. And then?

We removed our hands and it rose to the heavens, lighting the way.

One of my favorite pictures of all.

The Bible on relationships

I know it's hard to be the younger one, the one who watches from the doorway as older kids leave for friends' houses. With sisters 12 and 14 years older than me, I've been there. That's why it struck such a chord with me when Benjamin said he wanted to go somewhere that I couldn't see him.

He wanted to leave the house without Mom and Dad. He wanted to be big, and at 4, his options were limited. Then, it struck me: He could play on our enclosed front porch while I sat mere feet away in the living room. He could have the sense of playing just out of reach, and I could know he was safe because I could see him through the window.

He was beside himself when he heard the news. He raced around gathering up the supplies he would need to entertain himself. A write-on wipe-off board. A Bible. An imagination that somehow always finds its way back to Star Wars or Justice League heroes.

I could see him sipping from his mug, arranging things on the rustic coffee table and settling into the cushions on his favorite outdoor chair. He was proud of himself. You could tell it in the way he carried himself.

Within minutes he poked his head back inside the door. "I'm reading chapter one," he said, carrying his Bible. "It tells all about friendships… and relationships."

I started to explain how chapter one is about creation, but I stopped myself just in time for the reality of what he had said to sink in.

From start to finish, it is about relationships. Even the story of creation tells us God created man in his own image and then made woman, so they would not be alone. Then, God walked with them in the garden and delighted in their company.

And after the fall? Well, God still wanted relationship – that's what the rest of the book is about. The whole thing summarized.

Benjamin is a bigger, wiser boy, than I realized.

The Creator isn't afraid of stains

My favorite dishtowels are the ones that Mama makes. They're usually simple unbleached muslin with a healthy dose of hand embroidery.

Mama doesn't think her embroidery work is anything special, but when I wrapped my youngest son in one of her quilts and took him to the pediatrician's office, our nurse brought half the office in to see the handiwork. When my sister snuck around and entered one of Mama's pillowcases in the fair, she won second place without even knowing she was competing.

So, when she sent me a new set of days-of-the-week towels with some of my favorite flowers, I decided to use them only for decoration. I wanted them to remain forever free of stains. And that's exactly how it worked for about a year — until Mama came to visit.

This time she had tucked two other dishtowels in her suitcase, one with a bright yellow duck appliqued on it and another with purple pansies embroidered on it. I hung my favorite one, the one with purple pansies, on the stove handle where I could admire it and keep it safe, but in a flash it was gone. I found it crumpled up on the counter with splatters of chocolate cake batter.

Mama had used it.

If one of my boys had used my special towel, he would have gotten an ear full about all the work that had gone into creating that. Instead, I said nothing because it's hard to argue with the creator. Besides I knew what Mama's answer would have been. *I made them to be used and enjoyed.*

She's right, really. Too often I save things. I protect them and pull them out only on special occasions, afraid that my day-to-day life is too messy. *You can always bleach them*, she tells me. *The embroidery should still hold up.*

So, now I hang each of the hand embroidered dishtowels on the door of the refrigerator where little fingers covered in markers and dirt find the dishtowels a hundred times a day, and I remind myself that if the creator isn't afraid of stains maybe I shouldn't be either.

It has been a good lesson for me, not just in the kitchen, but in my soul because I think about my Creator and how faith isn't something designed to sit on a shelf or hang on a towel rack. It's meant to move into the messiest areas of our lives – and into the messiest areas of our society – to bring healing.

And I have to believe its most beautiful parts, its compassion and mercy, will hold up to the task because that's what it was meant to do. That's what its Creator had in mind when he created it.

Taking care of what scares us

That almost-man of mine, the one who turns 15 this month, he has a generous and helpful heart.

I've seen him bus tables for people in need of a Thanksgiving meal and bend down low to take his brother's hand and check a skinned knee. I've watched him spend his last dime to buy candy for someone else and take part of his vacation and feed animals that other people had given up on, animals that needed refuge.

The woman, the one who runs the refuge, she showed him how she prepares the food for the 250 exotic animals that were once pets. The tiger that was a Christmas gift for a 5-year-old. The peacock that previous owners found to be too loud. The turtle that grew too big.

We humans did this to them, she said as she doled out blueberries and chopped up melon. *We captured them. We made it so they don't know how to live in the wild. And now it's up to us to fix it.*

She patted a horse, greeted an iguana and fed two lemurs. When the gate closed behind us, I slipped in the question I'd been wanting to ask since I first heard about Safari's Sanctuary – the one where I ask how she takes care of the dangerous animals. The bears. The majestic lions. The alligators. The snakes.

How do you care for an animal like that, one that terrifies you?

Fear is often learned, she said. *And anytime I've been scratched or hurt, it has been my fault.* She misread the animal. She missed a cue.

She and Jessie walked ahead. I followed along but my mind was still processing how much of my own fear was natural and necessary – and how much fear I had simply taught myself. I choose to fear failure. I agree to worry about what people will think of my messy house, my rowdy boys and my written words. I use fear as an excuse for not helping more and that truth cuts as deep as a cougar's claw.

Fear is easier than faith. It makes it OK to pass on that rewarding job or that amazing volunteer opportunity. It stops us from pulling out the guitar or the paints or the running shoes.

Fear requires less but it also makes us less of who we were made to be.

We walked to the animals with the high fences and fierce teeth and all the while she talked about safety precautions and about love and responsibility. But no more talk of fear.

Leave it to love to see beauty

Forty one years ago – to the day – Mama walked in circles around what is now Tulsa Regional Hospital. Lap after lap in the scorching heat. Contraction after painful contraction in her lower back.

She had endured this pain twice before, but she did it one last time for me. This time, though, she swore she wasn't going to be suckered into buying expensive baby pictures at the hospital unless they were really flattering. She'd caved both times with my sisters. She'd be stronger this time, she said.

She wasn't.

She bought my stinkin' pictures, and they were the worst of all three of us. I had a difficult birth, so my right eye was almost swollen shut. I had scratches on my head and I still looked a little purple from the temporary lack of oxygen.

But I was beautiful, Mama said. How could she not buy the pictures?

Now we roll our eyes and we laugh. No objective viewer would ever see what Mama saw – or perhaps what she still sees. Leave it to love to see beauty.

She last wrote in my baby book when I was 27, and she still introduces me as her baby. She'll be one of the first to call me today to wish me a happy birthday and she'll want to know what we have planned.

I'll tell her we're getting ice cream because that's our little family tradition, and I'll say I wrote about her today – that she's in the paper. She'll chuckle and wonder why because she doesn't think of herself as remarkable. She doesn't know I could pick her hands out of a thousand, that I remember the time she was nervous about teaching a class at church and she invited me, a 7-year-old, to help her study.

She was just doing what mamas do, she'll say, and she'll remind me that she made lots of mistakes.

Ah, but leave it to love to see beauty.

We'll catch up on family news. We'll talk a little about the weather and what she'll need to pack when she comes to visit New York in the fall. Before she hangs up, she'll tell me that she loves me.

And I'll tell her I already know.

A grace-full dedication

On the day our two oldest sons were being dedicated, a wind storm knocked out power at our church. Suddenly, instead of electric guitars and drums, there was almost silence in a room of about 400 people.

Someone thought to bring out a couple of camping lanterns and put them near the pulpit while our pastor stalled for a few minutes, waiting for the power to come back on and our service to return to normal.

Still, nothing. So, he did something a little unusual for a Sunday morning: He asked if people would like to stand and share how God had blessed them.

There, in the darkness, they began to rise from their pews. One was thankful for help with finances. One was glad that God is helping her family make tough decisions. And several told how God had helped them through illnesses.

As each one of them spoke, it felt like the room got smaller, more intimate. By the time my little family went to the front, it seemed the world had stopped and given me a moment dipped in gratitude and grace.

By flashlight, the pastor read the words of the dedication ceremony. And it was perfect, especially for someone like me -- someone who too often allows the noise of everyday life to drown out the whispers of God.

Apparently I'm not alone, though. Many of the people who come to see Sue Staropoli are looking for ways to lead a quieter, more prayerful and balanced life.

"We're so activity focused," said Staropoli, a spiritual advisor in Penfield, NY, who teaches classes on contentment and taking better care of ourselves. "We under value the little things."

Like an act of kindness. Like a crimson leaf falling. Like the sound of a sleeping baby breathing in and breathing out.

We can take note of those things, she said. We can train ourselves to slow down. We can change our lives a moment at a time.

I'm ready.

What my husband's depression means for the rest of us

Can I tell you something about living with someone with depression? Can you draw your chair closer so I can whisper?

When one family member battles depression it becomes a battle for everyone else, too.

My husband isn't cranky or blue. He isn't even a glass-half-empty guy. But he does have bad days where dishes don't get done and laundry doesn't get put away. Where it's hard to pull himself out of bed. Where he fusses and starts a fight before we see his family for the holidays. Where he just doesn't have the energy for the fun day we had planned.

It makes the regular roller coaster of life have even more highs and lows, more tight curves where you feel slammed against the side of the coaster. And sometimes it makes it hard to catch your breath.

We show up late to events and appointments. We miss church. We limit the number of activities through the week – just to give us more margin, a chance to catch up if we need it.

It's hard on all of us, but we're all on this ride together. Brian is doing what he can. He's learning more about the illness, getting treatment and changing years of habits. And the rest of us?

We love him.

We love him in his brokenness just as he loves us in our brokenness.

Dealing with depression or cancer or diabetes is tough but **that's what love is made for.** *It wasn't meant to sell greeting cards, it was meant to greet us in our time of greatest need.*

When my daddy was dying of heart failure in a hospital room, Brian drove 1,200 miles to be with me and we had only been dating three weeks. And when we took foster parent classes and they told us all the behavioral challenges we might expect, I asked Brian if he was sure he wanted to do this because I had been the one pushing for adoption. His answer: God tells us to take care of the widows and the orphans, and he doesn't say to do it only if it's easy.

Is your chair still close?

This battle that we're fighting? It's OK. Love wins.

From nothing to everything

When hundreds of people you love live in one place, part of your heart is always there. Always scanning the Internet for news. Always waiting for friends and family to check in on Facebook to say that they've made it through the latest tornado or storm.

But this time, when wildfires spread through tens of thousands of acres in Oklahoma, a dear friend checked in with bad news. They had lost everything. All that was left was a twisted piece of metal that had once been their home.

Their 80 acres of beautiful trees once sheltered squirrels and bobcats, birds and deer. But in a flash, nothing was left but charred tree trunks and the ashes that fell like snow after the fire licked up the leaves and the underbrush. They had little warning and no insurance. She left with the flip-flops on her feet, some family pictures and her grandma's treasured ring.

The fire took the rest. The kitchen table. The senior yearbook. The shampoo. The security of knowing where she would sleep at night.

Still, even though I could hear the smoke fresh and heavy in her lungs, she was grateful. And she was convinced that somehow this was a blessing – that their lives had been saved for a reason and for a purpose.

Sure enough, as the hours ticked by more and more pieces of her puzzle came together. A relative offered a rent house he had been renovating. A friend opened her closet and pulled out nearly new towels. Strangers delivered an antique bedroom set, clothes and gift cards.

Just a week after she'd felt the heat of the flames I heard her say, *I have everything I need.* From nothing to everything in seven short days.

I'll try to remember that the next time the tears fall and my throat tightens with stress, the next time I'm feeling scared and unsure. If she can recover from a wildfire in seven days, surely my argument with my husband will be better by morning. Surely I'll find a way to get the house cleaned in time for a party. Surely I'll meet my deadline at work. Surely God – and his gracious people – will walk along side of me, too.

Parables and touching the unseeable

At our house, Benjamin is the great negotiator. When I say he can have one sip of sweet tea, he asks for two. When I explain that the game is over, he wants just one more turn. And when it's bedtime, it's the number of stories that we haggle over.

Books are fine during the day but at night he wants stories "just from your mouth." Often, he wants a loose rendition of The Three Little Pigs. (The building materials are changed from straw and brick to things like bubblegum and marshmallow, and sometimes Star Wars characters make cameo appearances at the pigs' houses.)

But it's the story of the three little girls that he asks for the most, a story that has remained structurally unchanged since my daddy started telling it more than 40 years ago, when there were fewer daughters to tell it to.

In the beginning, Daddy notices a pretty girl on the school bus. She's so shy that she rarely talks, but Daddy convinces her to go out with him on a date. And then another. Soon she asks Daddy to marry her – although, in fairness, Mama says it was Daddy who did the asking that cold December day in 1956.

Regardless of who asked whom, they decided to have a baby so they went to the hospital to get one. This is the place in the story where it gets really interactive. The listener must first guess the gender of the baby, then the name and then act out some of the things that babies do. This is repeated baby after baby until you wind up with me and what I consider a happy ending.

I've tried telling the story of the three little boys, complete with how I met my husband, but somehow Benjamin always goes back to Daddy's version. Maybe it's the cadence. Maybe it's the charm of taking a date to a drive-in movie theater. Or maybe Benjamin, who is just rounding the corner to 4, instinctively knows the power of a story told the way the Author intended for it to be. Maybe, like the rest of us, he's being carried by the twists and turns of a good parable to a place where he can touch the unseeable.

Running the good race

Some people naturally push the limits. Others, like my friend Kelly Nash, *shove* them.

She's run 5Ks and 10Ks, marathons and ultras. But she wanted something more: She wanted to run for 24 hours and raise $1,500 for the Heritage Christian Legacy Mile & 5K, an event that supports people with developmental disabilities.

So, more than a dozen of us – friends, family and co-workers – gathered to pray and cheer as she stepped on the treadmill the morning of that long run. We took pictures, sang about friendship and freedom and wondered silently what was limiting us, how we should be challenging ourselves.

Most of my decisions seem to fall back on what it will cost me. Do I really have the time? Is it worth the effort? But those aren't the questions that define Nash.

What if I just keep putting one foot in front of the other?

As part of her fundraiser, Nash rented out the treadmill next to her in 30-minute increments. One man, who was training for an upcoming half marathon, ran 13.1 miles with Nash.

"You'll have to train for a full marathon now," she said, still running. Still encouraging.

What if I really can go farther?

All of the 30-minute slots were full. They were taken by other runners; a friend of her dear, late father; her husband; her mother; her daughter's fifth-grade teacher.

So, she was never alone. Not when her eyes got heavy with sleep. Not when her body struggled to cool itself. Not when her fundraising edged closer to $3,000. And certainly not when she grew close to the 100-mile mark and to the finish.

Can I say I've run the good race?

More than 200 people, many of them still sweating from their own morning run, chanted Nash's name and counted down the seconds. When she threw her fist up in the air, the crowd went wild. The treadmill stopped at 106.49 miles. Four marathons in 24 hours.

I like to think she got her questions answered.

Hidden beauty – and safety

Even the drive to Meramec Caverns in the Ozarks was beautiful.

The main route was lined with trees that stretched over like canopy after green-leafed canopy.

Light danced on a tiny river to the left, the one that looked too small and sleepy to have cut through rock and soil and created a whole new world beneath the ground.

The boys unfolded themselves and poured out of the van, anxious for adventure.

Stay with me at all times, our tour guide told us. *I'll be turning lights on and off as we go, and I don't want people left in the dark.*

And so we began the easy, less intimidating part of the tour.

Larger rooms, lots of light. A bit of running water. A marker to show where *Lassie* had been filmed. A silhouette of outlaw Jesse James and one of his sidekicks.

Then, shorter ceilings. Less light. More guide-yourself-by-using-the-handrails, and finally a cul de sac where the group pooled to hear the guide.

The lights came on, and we were surrounded by stalactites and stalagmites.

We saw the occasional column where the two had met and melded their colors of rust and orange and dripping beige.

I drew in a quick breath, and I stopped listening to the tour guide.

This is what we'd been walking through in the dark.

These designs, hand painted by a loving and creative God, were inches away from the handrail.

They were just unseen until the tour guide flipped on the light.

Now remember the water in here is no more than 18 inches at its deepest point, the tour guide said, *but when we round this corner it will look much deeper because of the reflection.*

It is just an optical illusion, so don't be afraid.

The tour guide was right.

I could have sworn there was a deep canyon beneath the calm waters on the other side of the rail.

Apparently Benjamin thought so, too, because he moved his 5-year-old self away from the edge and to the middle of the walkway until the light shifted. Then he saw the truth, that the water he had been so afraid of would have barely covered his ankles.

And his mama got a glimpse of the truth, too.

Sometimes beauty and blessings — and even safety — are closer than I think.

God loves when we create

At our house even a conversation about monsters is never simple.

I had barely walked through the door when Benjamin showed me his drawings. There were six monsters of all different colors and all different abilities on one big page, and they were all fantastical.

He had talked his dad into taking dictation, so two of the monsters had names: Shadow Puppet and Reptiliat The Unchained, to be exact. And as he told me about them and their powers, he slipped in a question about God creating monsters.

"I don't know that God created monsters," I said. "I think that's something we came up with."

"With our imaginations," Benjamin said, more a statement than a question. Then, a thoughtful pause: "Do you think God minds that we made something up?"

My mind stuttered for a moment – or maybe it was my heart.

"I think God loves that we made something up," I told him before I pointed to our book about snowflakes, the one with close-up pictures of the intricate designs. "God loves to create."

Each snowflake is different and beautiful, I reminded him. Then there are the sunrises God paints fresh every morning and the shades of blue that decorate the oceans and the seas.

Benjamin beamed at the idea that he and God shared something in common, and I shook my head at how easily I forget. I put dishes and laundry and paycheck ahead of baking and doodling, ahead of crafting and journaling. I tell myself that those artistic things are things I can get to later, after the real work is done. I forget that creating was some of God's first work, some of his most important.

Busy people don't have time to write and send cards, to make their own bookshelves in their shops, to stitch love and warmth into a quilt. But in all that busyness, we've missed the sacredness in creating.

"In a sense, our creativity is none of our business," Julia Cameron tells us in *The Writer's Life*. "It is a given, not something to be aspired to. It is not an invention of our ego. It is, instead, a natural function of our soul."

A natural, and important, function of our soul. And something worth remembering.

How to thank the one who taught you about Jesus

For as long as I can remember, Brother Troy has had heart trouble. But now, in just the last month, cancer and its treatments make it so he can't stand behind the pulpit and deliver a full sermon. I heard he sat down halfway through his talk on Easter and that more hymns were sung than normal.

Of course the small Oklahoma congregation understands. Of course they pray for his strength and comfort. Of course they offer support to the man who has officiated at their children's weddings and helped them say their earthly goodbyes.

But it feels like there should be something more – some proper way to thank the man who baptized you and then coaxed you to wade deeper, to grow stronger.

In the more than 20 years that I sat under his teaching, I've lost count of the times the Baptist preacher told us that the name on the church sign didn't matter. *I don't care if the sign says Methodist or Lutheran or Pentecostal,* **he'd say.** *What matters is that they are preaching the Bible, that they are following God's teachings.*

Then, sometimes in the same sermon, he'd tell us not to just swallow his teachings whole. *Don't just take my word for it. Study it yourselves. Pray about it.*

I've always liked that about him, how he humbly points to God and to scripture – his true north. And I don't even have to ask. I know that hasn't changed in the years since I moved away.

His wife, Sister Betty, still teaches Sunday School. It was there in her classroom where my 7-year-old self fell in love with David and his psalms. Where I saw a re-enactment of Daniel in the lions' den on an old-fashioned flannel board. Where I memorized most of the scriptures that guide me today.

All those lessons. All those sermons. They've mattered in my life and in the lives of countless others. I'm in awe when I think about the influence of two faithful people in a tiny little town, and I'm struck by the far-reaching ripples of all people in ministry – be that behind a pulpit, in a classroom or mowing the lawn for a neighbor.

Thank you, Brother Troy. And you, too, Sister Betty. Thank you, all who teach us about God's love.

Dearest readers, Brother Troy went to be with his Heavenly Father in 2013. Many still mourn his passing. Will you join me in praying for them?

No one preached a finer funeral than Brother Troy. There was just something indescribable about how he shared God's love with those who were hurting. I'll never forget what he said at Daddy's funeral. He talked about faith, hope and love. He said faith and hope are realized in heaven, completed if you will, but love continues. There is no end, no death for love.

Much love to you, Brother Troy, and welcome home.

The legend of the rose rock

In Oklahoma, the Trail of Tears seems so recent, so close, that you can almost see the dust on walk-weary feet.

Our history books share the dates and explain the political reasoning but more powerful are the stories the grandparents tell, stories of how their aunts and uncles and cousins left tribal homes in the East and walked 1,200 miles to what was then Indian Territory.

They talk of sores, of typhus and cholera, of starvation, of homesickness and of death after death after death. Historians estimate the Cherokees alone lost 4,000 – more than 25 percent of the tribe – during the forced removals.

It's no wonder the trail became known for its tears.

But those stories passed down from Cherokee generation to Cherokee generation? They also tell of a legend of love, one that starts where the Trail of Tears ended.

As the story goes, God saw the suffering of the Cherokees and took note of each painful drop of blood and each heartbroken tear. And every time one fell, he took sandy crystals of barite and arranged them to look like a rose – a rose rock that blooms forever.

Nowhere else in the world is there a larger collection of these rose rocks than near Noble, Okla., what was once the heart of Indian Territory. They are still easily found in ditches and fields. Some are the size of your smallest fingernail while others are larger than your palm or have clusters of blooms, clusters of troubles.

When I search the red soil for them, they seem so fresh, so close to the surface. It's as if the legend continues, as if God never stopped marking and transforming the pain of his children – as if my tears over hurt feelings and your tears over past due bills and a sick loved one have been counted and captured, too.

I keep a small bowl full of rose rocks by my desk, a constant reminder of a constant God. They help me see that my God isn't some floating deity watching me from high above, but a God who walks with me step by step on my journey and turns my struggles into strength.

Those red-brown petals are symbols for me, a visual lesson of God's attentiveness. And when I grow weary or feel forgotten I try to remember that already the beautiful barite crystals are forming. Already God and his love are present.

Sugar or salt?

In my tiny Baptist church all the women contributed to potluck dinners and brought baked treats for Vacation Bible School, so I really don't remember who was responsible for the famous salt cookies.

I was young, probably under 10, and the cookies were set out on the refreshment table with the sugar cookies from other moms. It was just the luck of the draw that I happened to pick up one of the cookies sprinkled with salt and dip it in my red Kool-Aid. It was awful. Even worse than the time my cousin made me eat dirt.

The poor woman who made the cookies just grabbed the wrong canister. Salt and sugar, they look a lot alike but their purpose is very different. I tend to like my iced tea sweet, my strawberries syrupy and my religion nice and polite. Sugar makes things like medicine and injustice and poverty a little less bitter, a little easier to swallow. It hides the bite. Covers the distasteful problem.

And if left alone, sugar invites decay and disease.

I suspect that's why scripture says people of faith are to be salt and light. Salt brings out the individual flavor of everything it touches. It preserves and, even though it stings, it heals.

I've been dipping out of the sugar canister too often, worrying more about how it looks when my teenager rolls his eyes than about bringing healing to his hurts. I'd never pour sugar on his scraped leg, but I've scooped it in his hurting heart. Platitudes and syrupy religion rarely help, only salt. Only loving the unique qualities, strengthening them and preserving them.

I've read about human trafficking, child abuse and the need for more wells. Still, I take my sweetener and fill my children's pool twice a week with more clean water than some Africans see in a month.

I talk about getting my finances more in line with my beliefs, about finding more time to volunteer and more ways to speak up for others. But like a short-lived sugar high, I soon crash. I settle for complacency because it's more comfortable than being the woman who brings salt cookies when everyone expects sugar.

For the camera shy

When Colt turned 2, I had four or five pictures with both of us in them — two of those were family portraits. My track record with the other two boys wasn't much better.

And I take at least 2,600 pictures a year judging by how many I have saved on my computer. Five pictures out of 5,200 because I don't like how I look. Because every picture seems unflattering. Because. Because. Because.

Then, a few weeks ago I pulled out my daddy's wallet. I take it out of the drawer every so often, especially on the days that I miss him the most, and I flip through the pictures he carried. Us girls. The grandkids. We're all in there. And then, tucked away in the back is a single faded picture of his mama.

Every time he switched wallets, he moved that picture, and he carried it with him until the day he died.

She was that important to him.

All of us camera-shy mamas and dads, aunts and uncles? We're that important to our kids, too.

They love us with messy hair and no make-up. They love us in our raggedy around-the-house clothes. They love us and they want us in the picture.

Can you do that for them?

If you're in, will you encourage others by sharing your picture on the Simply Faithful Facebook page?

We can do this. For them.

The view from the curb

I remember taking walks on the quiet streets of Nevada, Mo., when I was freshman at Cottey College. My roommate and I would leave the suite we shared with eight other women and wander down to a nearby park, escaping calculus and statistics for an hour or so.

Usually by the time we were walking back, I could see lights on in the homes we passed. A TV would flicker in one house. A porch light would come on at another. If it was nice out, you could catch part of a family's dinner conversation through the window screen.

And it all looked divine to me.

If I could only get through college, start a career and family, then I'd have that warmth, that calm and loving routine, in a home of my own. In all my walks past those houses, I never once thought that maybe the TV was on to numb a painful marriage, or maybe the porch light was on to welcome someone home from a second job – a job that was needed to pay the mortgage. From the curb, and from my own naivety, I assumed that everything was fine in those cozy houses.

I know now that I was probably wrong, that life has a way of becoming complicated even when flowerbeds are properly groomed and sidewalks are freshly swept. Yet still today, I make the mistake of staying at the curb, of walking past when friends and neighbors are hurting behind closed doors.

It's messy, this idea of loving one another. It requires active involvement. It's risky, entangling and time consuming. But after all these years, it's time I learned the lesson. It's time I put it into practice.

Pruning to allow more light

For the second week in a row we went around the circle and introduced ourselves, told why we were interested in reading a novel about four women who meet on a spiritual retreat and why our hearts were pulled to discuss the book with others.

This woman had been there before, had driven the 45 minutes from outside Rochester to hear what we were learning from the characters and from our questions. But this time, as we told our names and our stories to the new people, she mentioned owning an apple orchard.

I told of my three crazy boys, of make-shift wrestling matches in the living room and of being suspicious of silence in our house. And once we were no longer strangers, we talked about "Sensible Shoes: A Story about the Spiritual Journey" and how we could see sticky notes and dog-eared pages in the books we held in our hands.

"What parts did you underline? What parts meant the most to you?" I asked.

One woman turned to page 15, where Hannah, one of the main characters, is being reminded of a sermon she preached about God pruning things like a gardener would. Hannah had told her congregation that pruning isn't punishment – it's improvement.

"I had never thought of that scripture that way," the woman said as others chimed in about pruning and its painfulness.

But the woman with the orchard shook her head and waited for a turn to speak.

Pruning is essential, she said, and we do it more than once a year because the trees need space. The fruit needs nutrients. *And pruning allows for more light.*

That last thought – the one about the light? That's the one that keeps ringing in my ears. That's the one that has me asking what I need to let go of so God and love and light can more easily find their way through my muddled mess.

Maybe it's my own expectations that could stand to be cut back or the binge watching on Netflix that could be trimmed a bit. Maybe I could take the scissors to my spending, my procrastination and a hundred other bad habits that pull time and nutrients from my soul.

57

The gardener knows with each snip, there would be room for more light and stronger growth.

Come alongside

I've always had an issue with textures. No chunky pecans in my cookies, please. No whipped cream in my hot chocolate. And, even though I love lemons, no slimy seeds in my drink.

Somehow, the other day, a lemon seed slipped past me. I didn't notice it until I took a sip of my water and saw it bobbing up and down near the surface. I poked my finger in but barely missed it. I must have touched the edge because it plunged toward the bottom. When it came back to the top, I tried the same thing again – and got the same disappointing result.

Of course, I thought. I needed to come at it from the side and then move underneath it so I could scoop it up.

One swift movement and it was out. Lemon seed crisis averted.

I had known better than to move in from above. It wasn't like the seed had a way to reach out to me and grab hold. But that's the first approach I used – and the second – and it's one I use far too often when dealing with people.

You didn't pick up your toys? You didn't finish your homework? You forgot to call the electrician?

Poke. Prod.

We're fond of saying we should only look down on people when we're helping them up but maybe we've got our directions all wrong. Maybe looking down on people wouldn't even be a temptation if we were walking side by side or if we were making it a habit to humbly lower ourselves in service to others – to be close enough to listen to one another.

Perhaps the 6-year-old is overwhelmed and doesn't know where to start cleaning the Lego-scattered floor. The 15-year-old might not have understood that math assignment, and the husband? Well, if I bother to ask, I might find that there are things besides rewiring the ceiling fan that are priorities in his life right now.

Instead of poking and prodding, I can always choose to come alongside. And from that angle, it's much easier to lift someone higher.

Our prayer tree

I sent the oldest out after dark to gather branches in the cold. Sent him with his coat and a vase and instructions to fill it with what looked dead – but would soon be made new.

He wandered back in, the branches still dripping from the melting snow, and I arranged them. Tallest in the back. The one that bent gracefully on the left. Then, I fussed some more.

I wadded up grocery bags and put them in the bottom of the vase and began arranging again.

Still awkward. Still sticks in a vase.

So, I set that aside and started in on the ribbons that would symbolize our prayers. First, the ones in all shades of brilliant blue and then the ones that looked like rainbows had swirled themselves across the threads.

How do you know how many ribbons you'll need? How many prayers will be whispered between now and Easter?

I put the first one on, one in blue for a little boy in Buffalo, NY, with a tumor gaining ground in his brain. Then, one in pink tipped with yellow for a friend with breast cancer. Jessie added one for his teacher who resigned and is struggling. And Benjamin grabbed a ribbon for the people in Oklahoma and in Joplin, Mo., who have picked through the rubble of tornadoes and pieced their lives back together.

I'm not sure who Colt, our youngest, prayed for. I didn't ask. My husband just lifted him up so he could drape a silent ribbon on a branch.

Throughout the days since, I've gone and slipped other ribbons on the branches, tied them with a simple knot and left my heart's request in the steady hands of God. With the addition of each ribbon, the sticks in the vase look less awkward, somehow transformed by the prayers that are covering them. And what was once a bit of an eyesore in our dining room has become the centerpiece.

I'm hoping the same is true for those we're praying for – that the dark places in their lives are filling with comfort and peace and even colorful joy. In fact, I'm hoping love and hope tie themselves in knots and cover us all.

What to do when bombs explode at the finish line

Moments after the bombs exploded in Boston, the questions started.

First, the ones that needed a quick response.

Where can I get help? What happened? Is my brother OK?

Then the questions that linger in a soul.

Why would anyone do this? How can I ever feel safe?

And the one that haunts me the most, the one that draws close to my face and looks me in the eye.

What can I do to help?

It taunts me every time another hurt flashes across my screen, every time I read of a too-soon funeral. Each time I feel small, too miniscule to do anything, so I fall into the carefully set trap of evil – the trap of thinking I can do nothing.

I pray and I pack my lunch for another day. I match socks and sweep dog hair off the floor. I begin to think that I'm right where evil wants me, defeated on the ground, and that's when something inside me starts to stir and kick at the dust.

I may not be able to keep the world safe, but I can give my children words to describe their emotions. I can model how to disagree respectfully. I can make the effort to not just know my neighbors' names but to know what they're going through.

I can turn off the TV and log off Facebook long enough to volunteer or send a thoughtful note or study something that helps me be a better advocate, a better voter, a better friend. I can live beneath my means so I have more to give.

I can do all of that and more because, make no mistake, hard times come to every neighborhood. From bombs in the back of moving trucks to tsunamis licking away the land, misery finds us all. And when it does, we need each other.

We need the candles lit and the signs hung that say we're in people's thoughts. We need the meals, the teddy bears, the memorials. We need to know that other people are standing – and kneeling – with us.

We need to know that God has not left us to deal with this alone.

I stare back at "What can I do to help?" and I start to nod. This, this is it. I can't prevent evil but I can work toward a healthier community, and when all seems dark and lonely, I can bring light and love.

That much I can do.

The rescue mission at the cross

As a parent, sometimes I don't always know the correct way to react.

The time Benjamin used red spray paint on my white washer and dryer I wanted to yell, but my husband explained that Benjamin had been trying to surprise us with a home makeover like the kind we watch on TV. I settled down pretty quickly once I realized Benjamin had kind intentions.

But a few weeks ago, I came in to the dining room and noticed something different about the crystal cross my mother-in-law gave us as a wedding gift. There, at the foot of the cross was a Star Wars Lego guy and more Lego guys were on the arms of the cross and at the very top.

I had no doubt whose toys these were – or who had placed the Lego guys there – but I wasn't sure what to think of mixing play things with a symbol of something sacred. Should I insist they be removed as a show of respect? Should I allow my boys more access to the cross so they could see the sacred as something approachable?

Before I had time to figure out how I felt, my Star-Wars-Lego-loving Benjamin strolled in to the dining room.

"Hey, do you know anything about what's going on over there at the cross?" I asked, nodding my head over toward the side table.

There was a small, impish grin and then the answer that turned everything on its head: "It's a rescue mission."

I think he went on to tell me something about Darth Vader chasing the good guys, but I really don't remember. I was too stunned by his comment, a comment that was overloaded and spilling with meaning.

Of course it was a rescue mission. Isn't that the whole point of the cross?

Bad guys, bad attitudes and bad hurts all chase us to the foot of the cross and sometimes it seems we aren't safe until we climb into the very arms of Jesus – the arms that are always strong and welcoming.

I didn't ask Benjamin to move his Lego guys.

I decided they were right where they needed to be.

Tuning in

It was the day I was supposed to write my column – two columns to be exact – so I could go on vacation and not have to worry about sending anything in to my editor.

And it was the day the old computer decided to work sometimes and not work other times. Like Pavlov's dog, I sat there in my home office waiting for my treat, waiting for the screen to blink on so I could peck out some sentences on my keyboard and check in on my social media sites.

But the minutes ticked by and no treat came. Not even a flicker. Not a post. Not a tweet.

I started shuffling papers and straightening books. I noticed Colt's tempera paint artwork and Benjamin's acrylic-on-canvas masterpieces, so I opened up a package of Command hooks and started eyeballing where the paintings would fit on the wall.

I dusted the bookcase, pushed the heavy Royal typewriter farther to the right and had Jessie bring in some trimmings from a friendly plant that lives in my neighbor's yard but likes to stretch out on our side of the fence. I pulled out Grandma's old cat eye glasses, some thread on a wooden spool and tiles from a Scrabble game. I talked and laughed with the boys while I brought out the markers and the colored pencils, the paintbrushes and the blending sticks.

All day we tinkered and visited and colored and decorated.

All day the computer made it difficult for me to log on but easier for me to connect. Because sometimes, when I'm checking in at all those virtual sites, I'm really checking *out*.

So, instead of spending those hours preparing for vacation, I spent those hours enjoying living here at home.

I warmed up the oven to make the boys' favorite banana bread and fiddled with those garage sale Scrabble tiles to figure out what I wanted to spell, what I wanted to remember from the day.

The letters were almost too easy to find in the pile: B.E. S.T.I.L.L.

A reminder of the day and a lesson for a lifetime.

Walking on sacred ground

When the oldest son came home talking about how he's studying terrorism in school, I didn't even wait until after dinner to pull out the pictures. I knew if I hesitated, I'd never tell him what it had been like that Wednesday in Oklahoma City.

He could get the facts from his teacher, but he needed to hear the story from me.

So, we started with pictures of a half-standing shell of a building and the thank you banners for rescuers that we all signed with our pens and our prayers. Then, the 168 empty chairs that became part of the official memorial, and the picture of the man walking solemnly along with his hat in his hands.

I tapped my finger on the man.

You see this? I asked Jessie. *You see how he treats this place as sacred?*

We all do, son, because love is there.

When our world was shattered, when we couldn't imagine a more painful or a more frightening time, love met us there. Right where the bomb had taken half the building. Right where the ground itself was broken.

Love came rushing in and gathered babies in its arms to carry them to safety. Love brought meal after meal to rescue teams. Love joined hands and held tight to those who were mourning.

When enough love is there, when it seeps in to the cracks and the crevices, broken ground becomes holy ground.

When a tiny nephew arrives too early, and a co-worker swerves too late. When your mama goes in for another surgery and comes out with no more answers. When that annoying mole on your head takes stitches and staples and introduces the word cancer to your medical file. When the car won't start and the dishes never end. When the whole earth shakes and tears beneath you, trust that love is rushing in.

And when it arrives?

Take off your shoes and know you are walking on sacred ground.

Standing shoulder to shoulder with your prayer request

Growing up in Oklahoma, I've seen my share of tornado damage. I know that brick homes can be reduced to rubble, that grass can be pulled from the soil – that once the winds calm, an emotional storm can start.

So, from the moment I heard a tornado had ripped through Joplin, Mo., I had prayed. For strength. For healing. For comfort. For peace.

And almost from the moment I heard, I knew I wanted to go there, to pray in the place where unruly winds had taken so much and so many. Six months later, we pulled off Interstate 44 just before the Oklahoma state line and turned onto the streets of Joplin.

Our van was full of boys and suitcases, of tired drivers and a barking dog. We desperately wanted our 1,200-mile road trip to end and our vacation with family to begin. But there's no arguing when the spirit is tugging.

First we passed what was left of Home Depot and its makeshift tent in the parking lot. Then, we saw signs that were leaning, businesses with blown out windows and homes that looked like they had tripped over their own foundations.

The boys had questions. What could do such a thing? Where do the people live now? Did anyone die?

We answered as best we could and then we walked to an empty cement slab and held hands and offered a simple prayer. The van was nearly silent as we drove out of town and back on to the interstate. We were each in our own worlds, each processing what we had seen.

By the time we reached the state line, the volume had risen again. The topic had changed, but the next time we prayed before a meal Benjamin remembered. And he has remembered every day, at every meal since then.

"Thank you for this food and help the people that got twisted," says the one who just turned 5. I never imagined he'd even remember pulling off the highway 10 months later, much less be continuing to pray. But standing shoulder to shoulder with your prayer request has a way of changing you no matter your age.

It makes it personal. It makes it real. And in Benjamin's case, it makes it lasting.

Making time for God

It flashed across my screen, this question about how to be closer to God when daily commitments are pulling and tugging at the seams of good intentions.

I thought at first maybe it was a question meant for someone else, someone who dutifully spends an hour each morning reading and praying. But she meant it for me, a mother whose house is rarely quiet and whose life is anything but routine, so I prayed and began my answer.

It starts with how we view time.

It's not a matter of carving out an hour to dedicate to God, it's about realizing that every hour belongs to him. Every moment and every task. The nine minutes after you hit the snooze button and roll over in bed, the commute to work, the hours spent typing or tinkering, the 10 minutes spent folding each load of laundry. That's his time, too.

You pray in the shower. You tuck a devotional in your purse. You put a Bible on your bookcase at work. You read books about faith to your children and listen to spiritual music while you wash dishes. You watch the ordinary unfold before your eyes and you search for the extraordinary, the thread that leads you back to God and his handiwork.

When you find God in those little moments, he becomes seamlessly part of your day.

I also like the idea of praying at certain times of the day, something I've seen while visiting the Trappist monks at the Abbey of the Genesee. I imagine it stitches the hours together and steadies the life. One of the monks suggested that those of us outside of the monastery set alarms on our telephones and computers – *that we use everyday objects to call us to prayer.*

And that pesky Ann Voskamp, a writer who makes it hard to splash around in shallow spiritual water, has been urging people to memorize scripture. I think secretly she's talking to me. I fell out of the habit of memorizing scriptures back in middle school, and I hadn't thought of it much until the author of "One Thousand Gifts" reminded us how important it is to commit words to memory, to heart.

I'll start my memorization work in January because this woman who asked the question, well, she's not alone in wanting to be closer to God.

God wastes nothing – not even our mistakes

I don't remember a time when Mama didn't start her day with a coke and a cigarette. She calls smoking her nasty habit, even as prescribed chemicals work their way through her veins to fight back the damage she's doing.

It's something she has done for 40 years now, a habit she just hasn't been able to kick. And she's learned to live with it. At home she uses vinegar to fight the smell, and when she visits we open all the windows on the porch and turn on the ceiling fan so the rest of us can sit with her without our eyes watering.

For the week or so that she's here, we don't even call it the porch. It's the smoke hole – the place where my boys can sneak in one-on-one time with Grandma. Jessie brings out his sketchpad, and Benjamin puts his Lego board on the floor and creates entire armies of ninjas. Colt pretends to be a dog and dances when he sees candy corn in my mama's outstretched hand. The whole time Mama is telling stories of my childhood, of how my middle sister refused to clean the fish tank, of how my grandmother came unglued when Grandpa trimmed her dog's hair so that he would look like a tiger.

The smoke swirls away. The ashtray fills, and I think of the advantages of this time with Mama on the porch.

My boys go in and out the front door, enjoying being in her company. Dirty dishes and sticky floors don't matter. They have her full attention from the time she lights the cigarette to when she snuffs the flame.

Sometimes I'm not even out there with them to see how they are getting too much sugar or to overhear what they are saying to a woman who is wise and adores them.

It's a level of independence that just can't be found enclosed in the living room.

So, Mama is right. Smoking is a nasty habit, but I'm starting to believe that God uses the whole of us and wastes nothing – not even our mistakes and shortcomings. I've spent a lifetime looking for gifts and strengths, forgetting that God offers beauty for ashes.

Even the ashes that are of our own making.

Dancing anyway

It was a morning when I already had a case built against my husband.

There was a list at least three pages long of things he hadn't done the way I wanted them – when I wanted them. Important things, like getting rid of that eyesore of an aquarium and taking millions of water bottles to the recycling bin.

So, I set off for work with this list running through my head and about the time I hit Lake Avenue I saw these three women out exercising. I probably wouldn't have noticed them except that they were dancing as they walked.

I smiled and thought it was nice that someone was having a good morning. And then, I had the little thought: *Maybe they've just decided to dance anyway.*

I pushed the thought aside. I had a lot to figure out before I made it to work, and I was hungry. There was that to think about, too.

Halfway to work, I pulled into a drive-thru and got out my wallet while I waited on the person in the car ahead of me to order.

I found no cash. No debit card. No credit card.

And I had no packed lunch for the day.

I turned the car around and drove home, sure to sigh heavily when I opened the door and asked my husband for the card. It was a simple miscommunication, but it meant my early-to-work day changed to a 15-minutes-late-to-work day.

I got back in my car and back on Lake Avenue and I saw the three women again. Their dancing had slowed a bit but they were still smiling and laughing. Good for them, I thought as I drove a little faster.

I was over a bridge and almost to halfway to work again when I noticed a man who looked like he was walking to work. As I passed him, though, I saw his head bobbing and his shoulders swaying. I caught him in my rearview mirror just to be sure.

Yes. He was dancing.

I rolled my eyes and took a deep breath. Maybe there's something to all this dancing – all this joy. Nobody's life hangs in the balance if I turn on my computer 15 minutes later than expected. I can love my husband even if the recycling takes another day, I thought.

So, I turned up the radio. And I chose joy.

Jesus' favorite

I was in the hallway of Woodcliff Hotel and Spa the first time I mentioned it. My husband and I had just been upgraded from a regular room to the Orient Suite – a difference of about $200 a night – and I made my confession right there by the elevators.

I know it doesn't seem theologically sound, but sometimes I feel like I'm really Jesus' favorite.

I said it in a half whisper then just in case anyone rounded the corner, but I'm saying it louder now because I've decided it's true.

A couple of weeks ago, the person in the car ahead of me at Tim Horton's paid for my bagel and sugar-infused coffee.

Clearly, Jesus likes me.

Then, something I had been struggling with at work came together better than I expected.

Are you noticing the same pattern I am?

A week later I had a terrible stomach bug. The worst I had had in at least seven years. And no one else in my family caught even a tiny bit of it.

Thank you, God.

My 12-year-old car? It's still running.

My family? Quirky and crazy – and loving and funny.

My refrigerator? Disorganized but full.

Sure, there are times when I don't get what I want or am certain I need. Times when I don't understand why God doesn't step in and tidy things up in this world and make it a little better for all of us, especially those in need of a safe place to even put a refrigerator.

But being his favorite doesn't mean having all the answers or always having things my way. It simply means I can trust his love for me in the thank-you times and in the no-thanks-I'd-rather-not times. *And it means I should reach out to his other favorites, the ones who – like me – he calls beloved.*

That mama trying to keep her daughter safe and off the war-torn streets. That man struggling to fight his way out of the bottle and into a job. That teen who can't seem to understand math no matter how many days he stays after school. That child who is scared and alone in the court system.

All of us beloved. All of us in need of God's strength and grace. All of us equal. All of us favorites.

Using what you've got to teach faith

Mama used to joke that I'd be the only bride who registered at junk stores for wedding gifts. I think that started after I found a pair of wooden theater seats tucked away in a store that looked like a chaotic indoor flea market. Or, now that I think about it, maybe she said that after I drug home that old Army chest.

Regardless, no one was surprised when I bought what looks like a shallow wooden basket and put it – chipping paint and all – on our coffee table. I, however, am surprised by how helpful it has been in talking with our family about faith.

I started by filling the basket with seasonal items and stringing a tiny banner made out of scrapbook paper across the handle. Within minutes, I found out that this was prime real estate in our house. Anything I put in the basket would be touched and read and rearranged by our boys. So, I started using the basket more purposefully.

In the spring I scoured the house for anything bee related and brought it to the coffee table, along with books on God and animals. Soon I'm planning to borrow the wooden fruit and vegetables from the boys' pretend kitchen and talk about what we learn about God from watching seeds grow and be harvested.

Eventually I want to pull together quiet bags that inspire questions and conversations much the same way the basket does – only in a portable fashion for those times when we find ourselves waiting or needing to be silent.

I also mix in storybook bibles and other faith-related books with the stacks of Star Wars and train titles we read, and religious music is in the rotation for family dinners. I write scriptures and prayer requests on the chalkboard in the kitchen.

If I want faith to be at the center of my family's lives, it helps for faith to be at the center of our home. So, I use what I have – even a wooden basket with chipping paint and crumbs of chalk – to teach and shape, to question and invite.

And I pray that God will take my chipped and broken efforts and use it all for his glory.

Morning always comes

It started three weeks ago with a loud thud, and by the sound of it, I wasn't sure what condition I'd find my husband in when I turned on the lights.

Thankfully, he had just missed one step and hadn't tumbled all the way down the stairs. But still, it was enough to send us to urgent care – and for them to send him home with a diagnosis of a fractured right ankle, which meant no driving.

Crutches for a stay-at-home dad who regularly grocery shops, cooks and cleans for a family of five. Orders to keep his leg propped up, even though we had planned a 2,400-mile road trip the following week.

And I was a mess.

I spent that weekend trying to figure out if we needed more toilet paper and what brand of sandwich bread we buy. I washed smelly socks, put away dishes and brought up board games so the littler boys could play gently with their dad.

We had almost made it to Monday when Benjamin started crying over a painful tooth. I went back to urgent care for a diagnosis of an abscessed tooth, a prescription for antibiotics and a directive to call the dentist. A couple of visits to the dentist's office and one pulled tooth later, Colt tripped and fell.

This time I gritted my teeth when the woman at urgent care asked if I needed help signing in. I've got it, I said as Colt held his sprained wrist.

We left with X-rays and a brace – and with Benjamin complaining that his head and stomach didn't feel right. This is the part where, if my life was a sitcom, the audience would start to laugh and the parents would rally and save the day.

Only I didn't want to laugh. I just wanted to cry and hide until my life returned to normal. Instead, I cleaned the van, got the boys settled in at home and went to bed a little early.

Then, finally, morning came.

Benjamin's stomach was better. Colt felt well enough to try to move his wrist, and I had a little glimpse of hope, a reminder that morning always comes even after the darkest of nights. It may take weeks, or months or even years, but light does break through.

And when morning comes? There's fresh mercy and grace for all of us.

How to have time to love your neighbors

Psst… I know you're busy. We all are.

We read books and magazine articles on how to simplify. We hire professional organizers and efficiency experts to help us squeeze the most out of every inch of every day.

It's hard to find time to visit with a neighbor or have coffee with a friend. And it takes time, *real* time to show people we love them.

So how do we do that? How do we add that to the steep pile of things still waiting to be done? We start by making it a priority.

Take three days and clock yourself. Where are you spending your time now?

Of course there are seasons in life – times when other circumstances make it difficult for you to have much control over your day. But is there room in your day to give a percentage back to God by showing love to others?

Even if you don't have a free hour in your week, could you combine some activities? When you are buying groceries for yourself, could you pick up a few items for your friend whose mother is in the hospital? When you do the laundry, can you pull out the clothes that are too small and drop them off at a resale store that benefits others? When you're waiting at the dentist's office, could you call or send a card to someone who is struggling? When you've got the lawn mower out, could you cut another yard?

And finally, once you've found extra bits of time, can you let go of perfection? Your sister – the one with a house full of the stomach bug – doesn't care if you made soup from scratch or if it came in a can. She just cares that she didn't have to make dinner and she likes knowing she's loved by you. She isn't looking for a Pinterest experience. She's hoping for a personal one. And you? You can do that.

Hospitality for introverts

I know there are people like me who feel drained after large gatherings. And people with the kind of depression that makes it almost impossible to plan ahead for social events. People with physical illnesses that make entertaining difficult, too.

Can I tell you something, all of us with our hands raised?

Hosting dinner is not the only way to love your neighbor. In fact, sometimes it's not even the best way.

It is the first thing I think of when hospitality is mentioned, though. The incredibly clean house. The perfect table settings. The food that all arrives at the table at the same time.

While all of that is beautiful and welcoming, it's hard to pull off with frequency – and especially difficult for people who struggle to push a vacuum or battle the throat-closing darkness of anxiety.

But there are other ways to invite people into friendship, other ways to support one another. Sometimes it's a phone call. A quick five minutes of checking in.

It could be a meal you just drop off for that new mom or for the college kid down the street. A ride to pick up a car from the repair shop. An offer to drive someone to the airport. A prayer. A chance to meet one-on-one. Maybe your friend stops by for coffee and cake on the porch. Maybe you meet out for dinner.

Showing love might be as simple as a bouquet of flowers from your garden. A load of laundry done. Fixing that flat tire on the kid's bike. What about those books weighing down your shelves? Is there one you know would be perfect to pass along to a friend? Could you visit www.littlefreelibrary.org and quietly start a Little Free Library where neighbors share books?

Maybe what someone needs is a kind note she can hang on her refrigerator – or a thoughtful letter he can tuck inside his jacket. Maybe someone needs to hear a compliment.

Whatever it is that you are good at, from painting murals to pickling radishes, that talent is important and useful because people need you. Just the way you are.

Tell your story

Few things are as important to me – or as sacred – as stories. I listened to stories before I could walk, and I told my own before I could read.

That's one of the reasons I enjoy this time of year. We gather around the table and retell the story of our faith. We share meals and memories.

But the truth is, sometimes I wish these conversations could go deeper. I wish we could get beyond the work-is-fine-and-the-kids-are-good answers. I wish we could know each other better. For several years I've made a living out of getting people to talk about themselves, so I thought I'd share some suggestions:

Always start with the easy questions, and then work your way up to open-ended questions. Pause. Give people a chance to collect their thoughts. Once they've answered, ask a follow-up question.

What interests you the most about social studies? Why is that band so important to you? What do you like most about gardening?

While they are answering, listen. Lean toward them. Look at them. Don't worry about what you are going to say next. It isn't about you. Just. Listen. Stay in one conversation at a time so you can focus – and that means putting away your phone, too.

If you disagree or if you don't understand, don't show it on your face. Give them the chance to explain themselves before you send a signal that you disapprove or you'll shut down the conversation before it really gets started. Then, if you'd genuinely like to learn more, ask respectful questions.

I've never thought of looking at immigration that way, could you tell me more? Could you walk me through an example?

Treat people as fascinating – because they are. And when it is your turn to talk about yourself, tell your story, too. People would really like to know what you remember about historical events. They do want to hear why you believe the way you do.

You'll all walk away from the table richer than before.

On Christian unity

Dear Christians,

I try never to exclude people, but today I'd like to focus only on you, the people who share my faith – the people I know best.

We've had a lot of disagreements in the past. Some of us have even split off from one another over doctrine and hurt feelings. And we haven't always been kind.

Many of us are convinced we have all the right answers, when in reality, we haven't asked enough of the right questions. We haven't asked and asked until we found common ground, until we found a way where we could work together.

We've used bumper sticker phrases like band-aids, but the scars from our arguments are still there. And those scars? They're distracting when we try to talk to people about love and mercy, about forgiveness and healing.

Belief has mystery all around its edges. We can use that to badger one another or to build one another.

I know I've wrestled with my faith. I've tested and tried. I've searched scripture and I've cried to God for answers. I suspect you have, too. Just because we disagree on things today doesn't mean we'll always disagree. *God never changes, but I pray I do.*

Clearly we have many battles to fight in this world, many causes we are called to support. **But we shouldn't confuse the number of battles with the number of enemies.**

There is only one enemy.

And the lie he tells us is that we are all enemies.

I hear it from the talking heads, the experts on TV. I read it in the newspapers and watch it scroll through on Facebook and Twitter. We act as if there is no hope for the left and for the right, and we forget – as one body – we share the same heart.

We forget that the baby in the manger came addressed to all of us.

We forget that God calls us beloved. Beloved liberal. Beloved conservative. Beloved sinners, all of us.

Beloved. Beloved. Beloved.

Jesus had kind words for prostitutes, thieves and murderers. He had harsh words for religious people who thought themselves better than others.

We have much to do, you and I. We must be up and about our Father's business – and his business is love.

I pray we can all agree on that.

The measure of a year

Leave it to C.S. Lewis to write things that chase and haunt me. That passage about describing light to people who had always lived in darkness? The one where he explains the same light falls on each of us? Yes, that one:

Is it not quite possible that they would imagine that, since they were all receiving the same light, and all reacting to it in the same way (i.e. all reflecting it), they would all look alike? Whereas you and I know that the light will in fact bring out, or show up, how different they are.

It's that last line I need on repeat.

Light brings out difference – and I spend most of my time trying to look the same, afraid of not measuring up.

As a mom who works outside the home, I read about the wonderful things home school moms and stay-at-home moms do and I make a mental mark on the doorframe. I'm not quite as tall as I thought.

I flip through the business pages and see people 10 years younger than I am who own their own businesses, who have climbed higher on the corporate ladder, and I make another mark.

"How am I doing?" I ask, with my back bent under the pressure of my own expectations.

Sometimes I feel so low and so small that I forget I was designed from the very beginning to be unique, to absorb and reflect God's light in my own way.

As long as I can remember, I've been in love with words. I use that gift in ways that I hope help people. My house is often messy and disorganized, but I try to take the time that's needed to really listen to my family – in a way that only I can. This has been an especially difficult year for me, one dotted with painful illnesses and heart-splitting deaths, and there has been spiritual growth that no marker can capture.

When I measure myself in that light, my back starts to slowly straighten, and I reach for the washcloth to wipe the doorframe clean.

Light expects differences, not comparisons. If we allow it, it brings out the radiance in me, in you, in each of us.

My prayer is that we'll all shine this year because we all matter and because we all have light to share.

When disability is part of the picture

When my mama talks about her third pregnancy, she always says that she knew something wasn't quite right. "It's nothing," my daddy would say — right up until the doctor saw that I was blue and fading fast.

Mama had been right. The umbilical chord was wrapped around my neck and arm, and I was choking.

As my parents tell it, the doctor never said a word or asked their opinions, he just reacted as a man sworn to save lives. He got me out as fast as he could, knowing that he might be causing nerve damage in my neck and arm.

Later, he would tell my parents that my arm might not ever grow or move on its own. "But, I figured you wanted her alive," he told them.

So, my parents took me home to my two older sisters and they waited and watched. Two months and three weeks later, I moved my right arm. I could move my wrist and wiggle my fingers, according to my baby book. By six months, I was crawling — not on all fours like most kids, but I could sit and scoot with my left arm. It was progress.

Eventually my arm did grow, although it's still a little shorter than the left. I can lift my right arm almost to my chin but my wrist seems to always be bent under a bit, something that has forever bothered me in photos.

One of my earliest memories is of having my picture taken in front of a wagon wheel that was almost as big as I was. The photographer had me rest my right arm on top of the wheel and then tried to flatten out my wrist. Within a second, it had bounced back into its U shape. She tried again. It bounced back.

The older I got, the more sensitive I became to being different — and the more determined I became to fit in. Of course, that's hard to do when you play trombone and have to use your foot to reach seventh position or when you have to swallow your pride and ask a classmate to sharpen your pencil because the sharpener is mounted too high on the wall. Still, I managed, and I even learned a little in the process.

Ironically though, I never knew what my birth injury was called until my late 20s, when pain in my arm made me seek out a specialist in Erb's palsy. While I was waiting for that appointment I wrestled with my arm in a new way. What if there was something that could be done now to help my arm?

Would I change it if I could? At almost 30, would I re-teach myself to tie my shoes? Would I discover that I'm not left-handed after all?

No, I decided.

I wouldn't.

I had my arm to thank for my entire world view — a set of values that helps me empathize with others; a set of values that says there are many ways other than the "normal" way.

Like Icy Sparks, a character in a novel by Gwyn Hyman Rubio, my difference has allowed me to flourish. Icy struggles with what she comes to learn is Tourette Syndrome, and in the epilogue she says that life would have been easier without it, "but I would not be me."

Years later, that book still sits upstairs in my office along with pictures I had taken of my wrist and arm — no longer in hiding, but out front in their rightful place. No portrait of me is complete without them.

My word for the year: start

My favorite journal is brown with antique maps wrapped around its cover. Just inside it carries a 2008 inscription from my husband. Words of love and encouragement. Words that urge me to "become intoxicated by the fragrance of every flower that makes up the beauty of (my) heart."

Beyond that is a blank page. And another, followed by another.

In seven years, my pen has never landed there, never rolled across the lines for fear my words wouldn't be sturdy enough to hold my expectations.

What if my penmanship was messy? What if all I could think of to write was a shopping list? How fragrant would those words be?

The edges are turning with age and thankfully I'm turning as well – toward beginning and enjoying.

I have a handful of resolutions for 2015, and they all fall under a one-word theme: *start*.

Start writing in the journal, even if it gets filled with ramblings and doodles.

Start the project I'm afraid I'll never be able to finish.

Start learning something new.

Start scheduling regular dates with my husband.

Start praying out loud for my kids.

Start kicking fear out the door, and start trusting that – whatever it is – God's got this.

Start acting like this life here is a gift, and I really don't have a moment to waste on worry or self-doubt or unforgiveness.

Start.

It's a good word, and I suspect it's a good way to come alive in 2015, a good step toward true faith.

That eloquent husband of mine, he likes a scene in one of the X-Men movies from more than a decade ago. One of the characters, Magneto, is crossing a dark abyss. At first, there is no bridge. No rope. Nothing. But when Magneto lifts his foot to take the first step, rocks rise and form a steady walkway. Each step after that – each *start* – brings more rocks for Magneto to walk on until he has safely crossed.

It's that way with faith, too, my husband tells me. We start and we trust, even without a visible pathway. Without all the answers. Without all the resources lined up in neat rows. Without knowing how we'll fill the page.

So, here's to having the faith to start in 2015.

Your dance matters

With a husband motivated to sample European cheeses and little boys itching to be outside, we found ourselves at the public market on a Saturday winding through the booths of apples and leeks and spicy pickles.

The crowd flowed by the bell peppers and the pineapples and the asparagus and eventually pooled in a small circle around a man singing and playing the guitar. A woman with red hair and bright blue leggings started to dance, her movements as wavy as her hair. Even though she drew our attention, she seemed to not need an audience. She seemed to just need to dance.

A little girl, I'm guessing about 6 years old, made her way closer to the musician. At first she swayed in her long, dark coat. Then, she danced, too. Sometimes she imitated the woman across from her, but mainly she moved her own way.

A toddler in a stroller started smiling and then waving his arms at the woman and the musician. And his mom sat next to him and tapped her feet.

Isn't it always this way?

One brave soul begins to dance and that gives others permission to take a chance, permission to be vulnerable and share their art. One man takes to the podium and shares with the world his dream of a day when all are equal and that gives others confidence and direction.

One mother says *no more* to addiction and abuse and generations are changed. One co-worker pulls up a chair and tells us we can do better than this I'm-rushing-but-I-can't-keep-up life, and we all sigh and relax our shoulders. We start to spend more time and money and grace on people.

One person issues the invitation and others, buoyed by her courage, begin to dance. It works in a group of millions, or hundreds or two because when we share – our art, our story, our truth, even our struggles – it strengthens us and our faith.

It reminds us we aren't alone and our dance matters.

It matters among the beets and the carrots at the market. It matters at home, in the coffee shop and in the cubicle. It matters in the pews, in the studio and in the seat of the tractor.

It's always this way. Your dance matters.

Love in action

I read their words once, and then again.

The first woman was responding to an article online about adopting children who are still healing from trauma. She was worn out from trying to keep a little one safe, trying to patiently enforce boundaries.

She worried that she didn't feel the warmth and lightness of love toward this child. Only duty. Only the humdrum motions of mothering.

Then – *and this is the important part* – in the next comment, a woman responded and said love is in the humdrum. Love is in the acts of service. Love is in the welcoming, the protecting and in the freely giving of yourself.

It seems we've fallen for the *feeling* of love. We are most comfortable with the butterflies and rainbows, the hearts with our initials scratched inside.

Without realizing it, we've put our confidence in an emotion that ebbs and flows. We've boarded a boat, and each time a wave comes, we doubt ourselves and the seriousness of our love.

But when see love as an action, as an expression of God, it serves as an anchor that steadies us. Even when the waves and the arguments and the hurt feelings come, love is still present in the scrubbing of the toilet, the punching of the time clock and in the tender holding of the hand.

Love is there when the rainbow fades and the paint gets scratched, when the hurting child acts out and you listen and hold tight.

Love is there.

Those people who come to weddings and adoption ceremonies and birthing rooms and tell you that all you need is love? They are right.

You need the action of love. The patience. The kindness. The humility. The showing up day after day after day.

That kind of priceless love is what you need for a strong friendship, or marriage or family. That kind of love will hold when you are bone-tired and broken. It will hold when you are afraid and so far away from your comfort zone that you worry you'll never find your way back.

It will hold. And it is all you – and any of us – need.

The accent of home

It was quick visit at home – just an extra two days in Oklahoma tacked on to a busy business trip – but it was long enough for me to start hearing that accent, that drawl in my head.

When I moved to Rochester in 1998, they tell me I talked like that, too.

One friend likes to joke that when he got on the elevator with me, it took me three floors to say, "Hi, my name is Marketta."

But there were other aspects of having an accent that weren't so funny.

I could be in the middle of a business meeting and have someone tell me, "Oh, that's so cute the way you say that. Say it again." Even worse was the time someone I supervised told me she just assumed that people who spoke slowly also thought slowly.

It became so frustrating that after a couple of years I started trying to hide it. I removed phrases like "fixin' to" and "going into town." I stopped saying ornery and cement and other words I knew I pronounced differently.

It was exhausting. If I'm honest, it still is. It is so much work to sand off the edges that make you different, so much effort to be like everyone else.

But when I return home to the place where my story began, to the people who loved me first, I exhale. I turn off the filter, and I fall into a comfortable cadence. I am simply myself.

I suspect it's that way for all us who wander and get distracted by what others think, those of us who grow up and leave the spiritual nest and forget just how much we – and our accents and quirks – are loved and cherished by God. We feel all alone and out of place but we have a place at the table, a place where we all belong.

Sometimes we need to go back there to be reminded, to be grounded in truth and confidence. Then, we can bring the accent of home back with us in our heads and in our hearts.

That all would be purer, braver and stronger

For years I've been a member of a group that raises money for women's education. We meet monthly, sometimes more, to discuss scholarships and low-interest loans and to hear the stories of women who are changing their families' lives, bringing business to their neighborhoods and solutions to the world.

Our seven founders – all students at Iowa Wesleyan College in the latter part of the 1800s – wanted to create a group built on true friendship. Now the Philanthropic Educational Organization has become a sisterhood of nearly 250,000 throughout the United States and Canada.

And all of those sisters? In all of those local chapters? They start their meetings the same way and with the same prayer: that all with whom we come in contact with will be purer, braver and stronger for having spent time with us.

That's a big prayer. A hard prayer. Leaving every one we meet in a better place than when we found them.

The kid with the runny nose who has asked for the iPad at least 28 times before noon. The woman at the Department of Motor Vehicles who tells you – even in the year 2015 – your debit card is not welcome there. That guy everyone brags about at work, you know which one I mean. The person who only likes things that are her idea.

Purer. Braver. Stronger.

That's an investment, friends. That's saying I'll recognize when a policy is out of your control. I'll see when you are hurting, when you are afraid. I'll listen to the whining and hear that you really don't need more technology, you just need more interaction and more time with me.

It means in the rush of the day, I'll take a moment to really see you. I'll choose compassion over completing my to-do list. I'll pick building you up instead of bullying you into doing what I want. I'll join like-minded sisters and raise millions to offer formal educations to thousands of women – and I'll know that the fundraising is the easy part.

Purer. Braver. Stronger.

That's where the real work lies. And there's plenty for all of us.

Many ways to wash feet

I must have been about 6 or 7 the first time I remember sitting in on our church's communion service. It was after the official Sunday morning service, after most of the casual visitors had left to see to their pot roasts, when the men slipped off their socks and the women pushed their dress shoes under the pew.

By the time our pastor began to break the bread, a sacred hush had fallen. When the grape juice passed in its simple water glass, all you could hear was the reminder: *Do this in remembrance of me.*

Then, one-by-one they knelt next to each other and washed their neighbor's feet. The man who had studied his Bible for decades washed the feet of

Daddy, who was new to faith. The woman who owned hundreds of acres knelt before someone just scraping by at the end of the month. There, with the towel and the basin, all those differences washed away.

And there was communion.

All these years later, I still count it as one of the holiest moments of my life – a moment where I saw God's love for all of us. While I can never recreate that memory, there are many ways to wash feet, many ways to serve one another. Many ways to do this in remembrance.

First, though, we must sit close enough to our neighbor to know her needs, so when she whispers that her very best friend is dying of cancer we can hear her above the din of our own busyness.

When we sit knee to knee, maybe we'll hear a single dad needs someone to babysit or a friend is overwhelmed and could use help preparing his taxes. Maybe we'll add a few extra tomato plants to share with an aunt whose arthritis makes gardening almost impossible.

Maybe we'll know who to add to our prayer lists – and we'll have people who are willing to pray for us. People willing to wash the dust from our feet. People willing to break bread with us in church and at home and at the ball field. People willing to remember God's love in the everyday, in the mundane and in crisis.

People willing to have communion.

A generous mirror

I never in my wildest dreams thought I would be surrounded by boys. I collected dolls. I made crafts. I liked dainty, vintage tea sets. I grew up with sisters, and all I wanted were girls.

Until I had boys.

What they say is true. They are loud, and they frequently wrestle after dinner. They talk of things like Minecraft and Star Wars. They wear holes in the knees of every pair of pants. They climb trees and require frequent trips to urgent care. And they are glorious.

In our tender moments, they dance with me in the kitchen and they ask me to marry them. They bring me flowers from the side of the road and they hug me and tell me it will be OK when I spill candy all over the floor. The younger ones take my hand in the movie theater, and sometimes even the teenager says he loves me when we are on the phone.

And on the days this mama feels less than her best? They provide a generous mirror, a way to see myself the way God does. They tell me I'm beautiful, or they wrap their arms around my neck and say that they've missed me all day. They think about the kind of video game I might enjoy playing – because they want to spend time together. They love me, and they forgive my faults.

None of us is perfect, of course, but that's when a generous mirror helps most. It's encouraging to be reminded that God and others still believe in you, that the people who know your heart see potential and not limitations.

Friends and cousins and co-workers. Sisters and husbands and mamas. We can all be a generous mirror for each other.

We can choose to tell one another that it will be OK. We can find ways to be together, and we can look for beauty. We can cut through our judgment and our unfair expectations and simply shine God's love.

And when we do? I think we'll all appreciate the view.

How to choose faith over fear

When Benjamin was 3, he asked for baby alligators for Christmas. Then, around the age of 5, he wanted a bat house for our back yard. And now, at 7, he's interested in having his own beehive.

Outwardly, I play the role of supportive and inquisitive mom but my husband can tell you how I threatened to put our home on the market four years ago when a bat got in our house and how last week I screamed and ran from a creepy silverfish that I promise was coming after me. But since Benjamin's interests are great and noble, I downplay my fear and try not to taint his opinion.

Fear is tragically contagious, and it can drain the joy out of life and take years to recover from. I don't want to be the one who introduces that in his life, or in the life of anyone else. That's why I reached out to Sweet Beez, a nonprofit that puts bee hives on roofs in the Rochester, NY, area, and asked if they might let a curious 7-year-old come see what they do.

A few weeks later we found ourselves with about a dozen people on top of a once-bustling warehouse tasting honey and listening to volunteers talk about the importance of bees. It turns out not all of their bees made it through the rough winter, so they would be adding new bees to a hive that night.

Would anybody like to put on a jacket and veil and help?

My son was the first to reach the jackets. A few other adults followed, but none got as close as Benjamin, who wore man-sized gloves that went well beyond his elbows and helped empty the bees out of their traveling case.

Bees flew all around his head and hundreds more buzzed mere inches from his fingers. But Benjamin wasn't shaken. He had listened to the seasoned beekeepers, and they told him he wouldn't get hurt if he put on the protective suit.

It made sense to him to trust those who really knew. It made sense to choose faith over fear.

I was glad we had come – and glad that confidence and courage are contagious, too.

Marketing Jesus

Turns out the talking heads – the ones who have studied us and written books about our behavior – say you and I aren't so interested in slick marketing anymore.

We're drawn to the imperfect. We think the video shot on your iPhone signals the message is more homegrown, less manufactured. Sure, we can still be pulled in by a glossy advertisement or just the right commercial, but in this over saturated world of ours the average Joe is looking for something authentic. Something real to believe in.

It makes sense, really. Who isn't drowning in a sea of communications, yet wanting at least a sip of something that truly matters?

But it's not just the creatives on Madison Avenue who pedal perfection. It's also people of faith, who in their earnestness to show God's greatness, pretend that everything is great. We put on our best dress or our most fashionable tie and we sell God and a beautiful, trouble-free lifestyle.

We forget that God doesn't need our polished marketing, he needs us to show our marks. Our scuffs. Our brokenness. He needs us to show how we've been redeemed. How he has knelt beside us and lifted us back to our feet. How he has taken our heart aches and our mistakes and made them beautiful.

Those cracks and splits are nothing to hide because they are really just openings for more of God's light and love to shine. They remind us that God isn't just available at the mountaintop, he is with us always.

When a bomb tore through the federal building in Oklahoma City and shattered the glass and the lives of those in the church next door, they hung banners all around that said *Our God reigns and we will remain*. Even with debris in the parking lot. Even with boards over their windows. Even with rescuers still swarming. Because if they had tried to clean up the mess first, they would have diluted the message.

If they had made everything seem great and glossy and trouble-free, the banners would have lost all meaning. And those talking heads are right. We all want something authentic, something that's true – in business and in faith.

When we show our scars and dents, we show the real work of God. We show that he loves us and gives us hope.

That's a good marketing plan.

God's got this

When Deb, a single mom, got phone calls from school or worried about the behavior of her daughter, she turned off the TV and she prayed. When her fiancé mysteriously wanted some time off from the relationship, Deb fasted. She read scripture and she pulled in as close to God as she could.

Every time she faced an obstacle, whether it was as scary as a potentially serious health issue or as simple as a looming deadline at work, she would turn toward God.

Every time she'd tell us *God's got this*.

She said it often enough that it became her trademark and the phrase we all held on to in the days and months after her car crash. At her funeral person after person told of her strong faith and her pure love and joy. And without planning it, person after person mentioned *God's got this* and they pointed to Deb's favorite Bible verse, which says that those who wait on the Lord will be strengthened. They will spread their wings and soar like eagles. They will run and not grow weary.

Deb knew about loss and knew what cancer could take from a family. She knew about divorce. She knew about hard work. But she also knew where her strength came from, or more accurately, who her strength came from.

And the best part?

She lived her life that way – as if she really trusted. With the little things and with the big. Without hanging posters on the walls of her office or wearing

T-shirts with Isaiah 40:31 emblazoned on them, we all knew about Deb's faith because we saw it every day.

God's got this.

I've grown to love that phrase in the last year. I use it when I'm crying in the drive-thru at Tim Horton's because I miss Daddy and when I'm nervous about speaking in front of people. When I'm afraid the teenager won't be ready for life beyond my house, and when the list of home repairs grows faster than my budget. When I start a project that's much, much larger than I've ever done before and when I look at a blank page and wonder how on Earth I'll ever do justice to my friend's memory.

Turns out she wrote her own story by how she lived: Whatever it is that we're worried about, God will help us through. We're never alone.

God's got this.

The secret to being perfect

Nancy Gullo will tell you she isn't a great gardener. She bought azaleas and put them in heavy shade, for goodness' sakes.

And she didn't spend much time decorating the old coffee can she has sitting on her bench in Bloomfield, NY. Just a simple white label that she wrote on in cursive: *Leave your prayers to be lifted to God.*

So, in her eyes, the sliver of her yard that touches the post office's parking lot isn't perfect, but it welcomes all of us even in our imperfection and brokenness. It offers a respite from the sun, the sweet scent of flowers and a place for a weary soul to rest.

It meets the need for hope and grace, and it meets that need now, today.

Gullo has a theory that if something like visiting a friend comes to mind more than once, she should probably go visit that friend. She shouldn't put it off or wait for an invitation.

I tend to hesitate. I want the right words for the sympathy card, the right recipe for the meal. *I worry and fret over being perfect when I should really be concerned about being punctual and about being present.*

Showing up at the right time to carry part of the burden. Showing up to say how proud I am of an accomplishment or a milestone. Showing up in time to grab my friend's hand and walk the road together.

I couldn't tell you much of what people said in the blur after Daddy died, but almost 14 years later, I still remember being surrounded by love and carried by the strength of others in the days and months that followed.

Gullo's garden is beautiful and serene, and it is perfect.

It's perfect for all those who have sat with heavy hearts and asked for the healthy delivery of a baby, for their husband to find work and for their friend to feel better.

It's perfect for the kid who wanted a prayer to pass a test and for the old biker who was thankful for a place to sit for a spell.

It's perfect because it's perfectly timed and perfectly placed.

When faith is inconvenient

A few weeks ago I was chopping carrots for soup while my mind stewed over hurts, over wounds and worries.

Slice.

I wasn't ready to forgive.

Slice.

How would this turn out for him two years from now? Twenty years from now?

Slice.

How many times must I, the one who knows what is best, reach out?

Slice.

I knew many of the answers, even before the questions were finished. Of course forgiveness matters as much for me as for the person I am angry with. Of course I need to trust God with today -- and with tomorrow. Still, I couldn't help but feel that day that real-life, practical faith was inconvenient.

I like faith better *in theory* and at a safe distance. I'll pray for those in prison and those far away who suffer from drug addictions. I'll talk all day long about the beauty of grace and God's love for all of us, and I will tell you how I love a great redemption story.

But can I be real honest here? Faith can be inconvenient when the one who needs grace and compassion lives in your home, when the one who hurt your feelings is a person you usually hug. And, yes, I love a good redemption story, but we broken and bruised humans can make a lot of mess before the story makes its turn for the better.

There, in the mess, is when it seems easier to walk away, more convenient to hold a grudge and tally the score. That's where I was that day chopping carrots.

I was right, and I had been wronged. I could teach him a lesson about his mistake, or I could show him how to live in grace and help him write his redemption story.

Slice.

I could be right or I could do what's right.

Slice.

By the time I moved on to chopping the celery, I had my answer: faith -- even though it was inconvenient. Because when it is most inconvenient, it is probably the most needed. For others and for me.

A lesson in leaning forward

At least once a day Colt pretends to be a train. He'll come running down the hall to my home office, his arms pumping like the side rods on a steam engine.

That's why I was surprised when he came up next to my chair and just marched in place.

"Look! I'm moving my legs but I'm not going anywhere. I'm stuck," he said, acting like he had a heavy trail of train cars behind him.

"Oh, Sugar, you have to lean forward," I said as Colt took off with a whistle through the hall and I returned to sorting through my notes and combing through my past mistakes. *Oh, Sugar, you have to lean forward to get anywhere uphill, to pull any weight.*

Could it be that simple? Does it really work that way with these two legs of mine and this one grand life?

It's simple physics, they tell me. We lean forward for better balance, a surer footing. And that makes me wonder, if I'm behind with my work or I've been a less-than stellar friend, can I really lean forward into forgiveness? If my relationship with the kid or the in-law or the neighbor has my stomach in knots, can I lean forward into love? If the chaos and burdens of the world ring in my ears, can I lean forward toward stillness and calm?

Sometimes I spend too much time looking back and worrying about the weight of those train cars, the regrets and the missteps. Or, I've been known to get distracted by what's beside me and I compare my mismatched furniture to what I see in the magazine spreads and I think I am the only one who can't remember which son has the dentist appointment today.

But moving forward requires looking forward. Even more than that, it requires putting your heart and your faith in what looks like a vulnerable position -- suspended momentarily over nothing but hard ground. Still, the physics and the metaphysics work.

A lesson for Colt, and a lesson for Mom.

Measuring yourself in love

I was in search of a gift bag when I found four yard sticks just to the right of the wrapping paper, leaning against a corner of the closet. Why would I have yard sticks tucked away like that, I wondered as I reached for them. Then I saw it: Doenges Brothers Ford stamped in black ink.

I remembered.

Daddy built his career at Doenges selling car parts and these two yard sticks had been at my parents' house since before I was born. When I was little, Daddy and I used to argue over who loved the other one the most. He'd throw his arms open -- about two yards wide -- and insist that he loved me this much and more.

The two other yard sticks sat for years in my grandma's sewing room and helped her piece together quilts that still warm my family today. As soon as I realized what they were, I put them in an oversized canning jar and propped them up next to my vintage telephone sign in my home office.

It was there that Colt came to me, still wearing the tiger's whiskers I had drawn on the night before, and asked me if I liked him just the way he was.

"I want to be like Benjamin," said the sweet boy about to turn 5, the sweet boy who wants every toy his older brother has.

Of course I love you just as you are, I told him as I scooped him up onto my lap. "God made only one you, and you are really special."

My hugs and my words seemed to comfort him. It was enough, for now, that I said he was valuable -- that he measured up just the way he was.

And there, in the shadow of the yard sticks, I felt it, too. There is a sense of relief when you know the ruler you're being measured by is owned by the One who loves you. One who has seen you at your worst and at your neediest and still chooses you, still calls you beloved. One you can trust.

I knew then that I'd leave the yard sticks out for a while because we all need a reminder of our worth and a reminder of whose measurements really matter.

For when you need to be overwhelmed by grace

For almost two years I talked to the boys about the Great Salt Plains in Oklahoma — how we would leave the trees and hills of Tulsa and trade them for the red dirt and flat, fertile plains to the west.

I described to them how you can watch a thunder storm careen across the sky for miles without buildings and lights spoiling the view and how, when we got to the salt plains, we would see the white stretch out all the way to the horizon.

Still, when the dirt road ended and we passed through the gate, they weren't sure what to make if all that salt. It was overwhelming.

We brought out our borrowed shovel and began to dig shallow holes. We poured water down the sides and caught glimpses of sparkling crystals. The boys filled one plastic cup with treasures and started on another while I looked at their smudged faces and their shoes caked with mud and salt.

Our tires were white.

The knees of Jessie's black jeans were white.

Everything was white because there was an abundance of salt. Not a salt shaker full, acres and acres full.

The Christian scriptures tell us that people of faith are to be light and salt in this world, and in all these years that I've been reading that verse, I've pictured salt on my dinner table. I've thought about salt's importance in preserving and seasoning, but I've visualized it as small and scarce.

I forgot that it fills oceans and seas and mines — even a portion of the plains in my home state.

I forgot that there is plenty of salt for purity, for sharing the flavor of compassion and grace. If we want, the salt that was once used to bind people in an unbreakable covenant of friendship could overflow on our tables and in our lives.

And the light that shines in darkness? The symbol of God's love and hope? It's plentiful, too, year after year after year.

That changes things for me. It shifts my thinking and my fears.

Unlimited love. Hope. Purity. Healing. Grace.

And suddenly, like the boys, I'm overwhelmed.

EASTER COLUMNS

The ugly clay foot

I've seen mosaics with gilded halos around the heads of saints and stained glass windows that stretched 20 feet or more, glowing with light. I've stood within a breath of Michelangelo's *la Pieta*, and I still remember how no detail was rushed or skipped – every muscle, every vein captured there in marble.

And now, I've seen the ugly clay foot in my friend Linda Gordon's car.

I'll admit, I wasn't sure what it was when I first leaned over to buckle my seatbelt. I just saw it out of the corner of my eye, sitting there taped to the dashboard by the clock. It was an inch and a half, 2 inches at most. Pinkish, like my skin, and it had one slightly chipped toe courtesy of an unfortunate fall to the floorboard of the Kia.

I took in a quick breath before I blurted out, "What is that?"

"It's a foot," she said, as if it were the most common thing in the world.

She had gotten it at church in the days leading up to Easter. She had her choice among a rooster, some silver coins or a foot – all reminders of Jesus' final days before his crucifixion.

The rooster was kind of big and unattractive, she said, with a shrug, so she went with the small, ugly foot.

"I painted its toenails after it fell," she said, as she backed out of her driveway. "I think it looks a lot better now."

It was hard to argue. She had done a terrific job painting the toenails a shade of cotton candy pink.

"It reminds me that we're all on a journey," she said, the foot bobbing just a tiny bit on top of its loop of tape. It was slightly unconventional, and certainly unexpected, but there it was: Her very own quirky religious symbol.

I still like ornate crosses and finely detailed nativity scenes, but I began to see the awkward clay foot in a slightly different light. Take the next step in faith. Walk with God. Add beauty on the journey, it seemed to say.

"Do you think I could get my own foot for my dashboard?" I asked.

She promised to ask if there were any left over at church. "But you'll want to paint the toenails," she advised.

Of course.

May the stone be rolled away

I never understood the full symbolism of winter until I moved to Rochester. I grew up in a place where it got plenty cold, but usually for just a few days or a week at the most.

Even when we were bundled in our winter coats the sun was shining almost every day, and snow was an excuse to stay home by the fire and throw snowballs with the neighbor's kid.

Winter was just a break from mowing the grass and watching for rattlesnakes. It wasn't anything I thought about enduring or rushing through until I had my first late February and early March here, when spring and rebirth couldn't come fast enough.

I was desperate to go outside without gloves, to see some sign of life coming out of the soil – to finally have light and warmth.

Now, I understand when people say they are living through winter in their lives. I know about darkness and gray. I know how snow and bills and medical concerns can pile up and block your view.

I know how it can look like the end.

In the Christian tradition we're beginning to celebrate Lent this week and we'll follow along in our scriptures as Jesus ministers, is adored by the crowds and then faces his own winter, his own suffering and death.

His followers were, of course, unsure what to do. Worried about their own safety. And so very sad and heartbroken. But scripture tells us that on the third day some of the women who were closest to Jesus went to his sealed grave and found that the stone – the one specifically chosen because it was so difficult to move – had been rolled away and Jesus had risen from the dead.

Spring and light had come after all.

As we prepare for Easter this year, my prayer for us is that whatever heavy boulders are blocking new life will be rolled away.

Self doubt. Fear. Pride. Addiction.

May it all be moved so we can be alive and free.

For when it's hard to wait

When I finally remembered to buy seeds for wheat grass, I did what I typically do: I went a bit overboard.

How was I supposed to know that a measly pound of seeds would take care of the jungle Benjamin was planning for his LEGO guys, the tall grass scene Colt insisted on planting in the cigar box, my decorations for Easter and much, much more?

I soon ran out of proper pots, so I lined a thrift-store basket with a plastic grocery bag and planted there as well.

And still there were seeds.

I did what any practical person would do and pulled jars out of the recycling bin to serve as see-through planters. I told myself it would be a great learning experience for the two younger boys, a chance to see nature at work, but I found I was drawn to the jars even more than they were.

I checked them almost every time I walked past. It seemed like nothing was happening in the other, prettier pots, but I noticed every new sprout in the jars. When the roots started unfolding I made everyone in the house come look.

Because I could see what was happening beneath the soil, I knew it was just a matter of hours before the first bits of green would break through. It was easy, exciting even, to wait.

It was hard to imagine the same thing happening in the more traditional pots, the places where I had to rely on faith instead of sight. I knew – really knew – that the same process was happening in both places, but I like tangible results in my gardening and in my prayer life. Results I can see and track and check up on. Results that aren't buried beneath soil or hidden in hearts.

God, that person I'm having a hard time with, you're going to help me with that right? And my desire to be more positive and to be a better wife? You haven't forgotten about that?

The green tips of the wheat grass did break through in all the pots, the basket, the jars, the jungle and even the cigar box. They moved shyly at first, barely seen, but as the soil split to make room for the new, I had my evidence. Blade after beautiful blade.

And even in the dark, away from my eyes, seeds of faith were growing.

CHRISTMAS COLUMNS

Making Christmas welcoming to all

Somewhere around the middle of November I start to brace myself. I love the holidays but they aren't always kind to my family.

When I send our oldest son off to school, he offers a weary smile – a sure sign of another sleepless night spent with memories of birthdays and Christmases before his adoption.

Then, there's the man I married who hasn't heard from his biological father in more than 30 years. While perfect families flash smiles across the screens, he fights off the questioning and the wondering that's always chasing him this time of year.

My job is usually to comfort them, to reassure them that they are loved and valued, and to keep the holidays normal for the two younger boys. I wrap presents and drape strings of pearls on the tree. I make hot chocolate and search for the best neighborhood light displays. I stay home and feather the nest.

I've gotten pretty good at it, so we look OK from the outside. But I've been angry inside. Troubled that the people I love have been hurt. Upset that some of their joy has been stolen. Burdened by the thought that Christmas doesn't feel very welcoming to them.

So this year I'm reading the Christmas story differently. And in the process, we're rewriting our own.

I'm elbowing in at the manger, knowing that Jesus welcomes everyone. The grieving. The sick. The financially strapped. The less-than-perfect and the far-from-perfect.

I'm sidling up beside Mary and Joseph who know what it's like to have a family that's different from everyone else's and what it's like to have your own plans changed.

I'm standing shoulder to shoulder with the shepherds who are desperately seeking light in the darkness, who have come in their dusty shoes for the promise of peace.

Oh, how I'd like to get that angel's attention. I desperately want to be close enough to whisper: *Please, continue to tell the good news. Light up the sky and invite people to come as they are to Christmas. Remind them that they aren't alone in this crazy life and that there's plenty of room – and love – here at the manger.*

And I pray that the sacred, almost indescribable joy of Christmas comes to hearts both whole and broken this season. It's meant as a gift for all.

Celebrating all of Christmas

Growing up with Erb's Palsy, I often had to ask for help with the little things – the things that would be much easier with two good arms:

French-braiding my hair.

Sharpening my pencils in class.

Fastening necklaces.

By now you'd think I'd be used to it. After all, the nerve damage in my neck and right arm was caused at birth. I've never known what it was like to be able to raise my right arm or straighten my wrist.

I was 12 before I figured out a way to put on a pair of pantyhose without help from my mama, and my middle sister drove two hours to hang pictures and curtains in my first apartment. My daddy cut my steak into bite-sized pieces for me the first 29 years of my life, and now my husband discretely slides my plate over at restaurants to do the same.

Still, after all these years, I blush. I'm embarrassed that I need help at all.

I think that's pretty common, the desire to feel like you have it all together, that you don't need anything from anyone else – that you are the giver, not the receiver.

In fact we celebrate that idea throughout the end of each year. We gather food baskets for those deemed "needy" and we wrap Christmas gifts for those who are "less fortunate." We buy presents for our kids, our mailman and our hair stylist because it is, after all, the season of giving.

But is that how it was meant to be? Did God intend for us to give gifts or did he mean for us to accept his gift, the present of love and joy that he wrapped in swaddling clothes and put in a manger?

I suspect he wants us to do both – to experience the feeling of helping others and to know what it is like to be the one who needs a lift. It's humbling to know that I stumble on my own and must rely on God's wisdom and grace and the kind shoulders of family and friends. I'd rather focus on being the giver, but that would be celebrating only half of Christmas.

When Jesus goes missing from the nativity scene

It started innocently enough, this idea to let the boys play with a plastic nativity set. I thought it would be a nice distraction while we read Christmas books and a chance to reinforce the story of Jesus' birth. But before we made it through the first few pages, there was trouble.

I did the parental nod toward my husband and subtly shifted my eyes over to Colt, our youngest son, who had an angel hanging out of his mouth and was shaking his head from side to side. I tried to not make a big deal out of it since it was family time – a time when we generally try to stay positive. So, we kept reading until our middle son, Benjamin, swiped a donkey and a shepherd from our oldest son.

I barely had time to lecture Benjamin on the need to share before I saw him knocking over the wise men and heading for the baby Jesus to get the other bad guys.

"Let's not use Jesus for violence," I said. "That's not the kind of thing he teaches."

A few more pages and the book ended. We pulled out the words to *The Friendly Beasts*, an old Christmas carol that talks about the gifts the animals brought to baby Jesus, and we took out wooden figures that the boys could use to act out the song. Somewhere between the cow offering her manger and the sheep bringing wool for a blanket, I noticed blue swaddling clothes hanging out of Colt's mouth. I did the infamous finger sweep.

"You can't chew on Jesus," I told him while I checked for teeth marks in the wood. Thankfully there were none, so I wiped off Jesus and put him back in the manger. He was only there for a few seconds before he went missing.

"Great," I said, less than thrilled. "Where is Jesus?"

Then, I saw him. There, in the middle of the scattered Fisher Price nativity set and the jumbled wooden figures, was our Jesus in blue swaddling clothes.

Right there in the chaos of my little family. Unfazed and solid as ever.

"Can we play again tomorrow?" Benjamin asked.

"Absolutely," I said. "Absolutely."

An invitation to Christmas – and every day

Hey, you.

Feeling rushed and so very far behind? Calculating and recalculating your black-to-red checkbook balance? Not sure what you're putting on the dinner table tonight?

Is that you?

Beating yourself up for your lack of patience this morning when the kids dawdled or blood pressure still rising because the car in front of you wouldn't turn right on red? Ashamed of that thing in your past, the one you don't want anyone to hear about? Tired – and ready to give up – from the hard hits of life?

Is that you?

Feeling small and less than? Feeling torn apart instead of feeling a part of Christmas? Wondering how a babe in a manger means anything in this crazy world? Asking why he bothered to come at all?

Is that you?

Can I start by telling you that the babe in a manger is comfortable with questions? Did I mention that he doesn't expect you to have it all figured out? He came to a tiny town to be born in a place where there wasn't even room for him, right? Maybe he knows a little something about feeling like things aren't ready? About feeling pushed to the side in the chaos?

And do you think that innocent babe knows nothing of sin and hurts and forgiveness? Did you forget that he grew to dine at the home of a shady tax collector and hang by the side of a thief? Could it be that he understands all our shades of brokenness and offers mercy anyway?

What if he doesn't rescue us from every hard thing but walks with us – never leaving our side? What if he feels every one of those hard hits with you? Wouldn't that make sense when he tells us he collects every tear and saves them? Knows the number of hairs on our heads?

Can you imagine how much he wants to draw us near to the manger and offer his peace? Maybe bring a bit of stillness and wonder to our days, make each of them holy?

Might I suggest that this God of grace comes looking for you right where you are? How could he not search for you and invite you to come closer? Didn't he call you beloved? Say you were cherished and chosen? Loved without measure?

Is that you?

That's you. That's really you.

And you are welcome at Christmas – welcome always.

OTHER HOLIDAY COLUMNS

A letter for MLK Day

My sons and those of your generation,

You will grow up reading about the Rev. Dr. Martin Luther King Jr. in your history books. You will visit museums where "whites only" signs will hang behind glass, where you watch grainy footage of crosses being burned in yards.

But sons?

Please don't make the mistake of assuming this is ancient history. Not all things that are housed in museums are old or far removed from today.

Your grandmother remembers when kids who were black were first allowed to come to her high school. Your grandmother who is not even 80.

I have a friend who still cries when she talks about not being able to walk through white neighborhoods or use certain restrooms. This isn't ancient history for her, sons. The wound is still fresh.

We can't turn the page or go to the next exhibit and forget this because we will be tested on it. We will be graded on what we have learned from this. And this exam matters. It matters tremendously.

So, sons, my hope for you is that you always use your strength for those who are weak, for those who don't have power or pull. My hope for you is that you'll be so generous that you'll be thought foolish – because anything less is not enough.

And boys, always extend the welcome. Look around and seek out those who are quiet or not there. Which voices are missing? I know it's not popular to invite the outsider, but God invites all of us. Never forget that.

No matter how old you are, watch your language because it's not just curse words that are foul. Jokes are often a Trojan horse for stereotypes, assumptions and put-downs. What you allow yourself to say – even in jest – you allow yourself to believe.

Soon enough you'll come upon a situation where you aren't sure what the right answer is or how you should re-act. When in doubt, choose love. It really is the right answer to almost any question.

Take these lessons and carry them forward, sons. You are writing the history books for your children and for theirs. May it be a history of progress.

A message for the women who love

Hey, mothers. Moms. Aunts and cousins and friends who do your very best to nurture others.

I hope all the people you love made you feel special this Mother's Day. I hope they held the door open for you, pampered you with your favorite foods and hugged your neck until it was hard to breathe – both because of the closeness and because of the joy.

But I hope one thing above all: I hope this time you listened and started to believe you really are good at mothering.

Oh, I know what you're thinking. You're OK at this gig, but you mess up a lot. You get impatient. You let them watch too much TV. You aren't as consistent with bedtime as you need to be. You need to find more ways to connect.

All of that may be absolutely true. Remember, though, that mothering doesn't come with a checklist or a scorecard. Instead, it comes with its own share of grace.

So, when that 3-year-old calls you his friend and the 6-year-old says he is impressed with your beauty? Smile. Say thank you. And believe the truth. You are cherished, and you were chosen for this family, for these very people.

Sure, hard times will come, times that test those ties. But don't assume that's because of bad mothering. We all make mistakes, and sometimes it's a mistake to blame ourselves.

So many of us have fallen in this trap of always feeling guilty, always feeling less than. We think this is humility. We think this is how we push ourselves to get better.

But friends? May I cup my hand under your chin and lift your head higher for a moment? Let me look you in the eyes and tell you this.

Beating yourself up doesn't make you better. It just keeps you down.

If you want to improve for God, for yourself, for the people you love, then it's grace you need. Grace speaks to your soul and whispers that you are forgiven. Grace puts its arms under yours and lifts you back to your feet. Grace dusts you off and sets you free to be the woman you were meant to be.

God's grace is sufficient for you, lovely mama. It's sufficient for you, dear aunt. It's sufficient for all of us.

Now, go in peace and in confidence. Do the work you are called to do.

Father's Day for the man I married

If my math is right, I write more than 22,000 words a year here in this space. I tell you about my struggles and my prayers. I share stories about my past, and let's face it, you've practically watched my boys grown up here in these lines.

But I've told you very little about my husband, Brian.

Maybe you remember he's a Navy veteran and that he fights depression. Maybe you know he agreed to adopt our oldest son before he ever met him. Maybe you've seen his handsome face on my blog or on social media.

And maybe it's time I told you more.

I met him while writing a story, and I think he asked me just as many questions as I asked him. We had been dating for three weeks when Daddy had a heart attack and I flew to Oklahoma to be there for his bypass surgery.

I showed him a picture of Brian and his broad shoulders and I told Daddy this guy was different.

I know, Daddy said. *I can tell.*

We were married a year and a half later.

Our dedication – and our fights over paint colors, money and household chores – grew as we started our life together as husband and wife. Then, because living with one person isn't complicated enough, we added children.

I've always believed you can glimpse a person's true character by watching how he treats children, how he cares for those who hold the least power.

I've seen Brian's notes on the kitchen counter, the ones he scratches out late at night when he's thinking about what's important for our boys to learn and the best ways for them to learn it. I've heard him apologize to the boys and watched him model how to argue without calling names, how to stand up for the people you love, how to sit with someone who is hurting and how to pray.

He reads Edgar Allen Poe with the teenager, Star Wars books to the 6-year-old and model train catalogs to the 3-year-old. He has been known to wrestle with the boys after dinner, explode pop bottles and use the vacuum hose to style the littlest guy's hair.

All of that silliness is good for us, and so is the way he keeps us steady. We're thankful for him and for all the men whose character shines. Today and every day.

Sailor's tour continues

I never knew my husband when he was on active duty in the military. I've only seen pictures of him wearing the standard sailor's hat, the navy and white uniform.

He claims I wouldn't have liked him much then, with his foul mouth and teenaged angst, but I can't imagine meeting him and not falling in love -- at any age.

When we were planning our honeymoon, I suggested a cruise and he cringed. I had visions of sunbathing on the deck and dancing at night.

He had visions of being out to sea for six months and working almost non-stop painting and repairing airplanes.

The first time we visited my family in Oklahoma, he pulled out his military duffle bag and began rolling enough shirts, pants and shoes for weeks. Then he squeezed in towels, a Brita water pitcher and filter and what seemed like 20 other things.

Nobody packs for a trip like a veteran.

Brian will sometimes show our boys online videos of what sailors do the first time they cross the equator or he'll talk about how tricky it is to get an aircraft carrier safely through the Suez Canal. But he never talks about the three airplanes he saw crash into the water or about how he still wonders 17 years later if there was something he could have done better as an airplane mechanic.

I didn't know about the crashes until we were closing in on our eighth wedding anniversary. Brian was having some medical and educational testing done and one of the questionnaires touched on traumatic events.

If the doctor hadn't referenced the airplane crashes in his report, I probably still wouldn't know about them.

I'd continue buying Brian a card on Veterans Day and thanking him on the Fourth of July, and I wouldn't realize that his tour of duty isn't quite done.

Like so many other men and women, he has the paperwork, the formal discharge and the medals – and still he carries a heavy weight. Still he serves.

Our veterans may be out of harm's way. They may have made it safely home. But they still need our prayers and they deserve our thanks for a lifetime of service.

INDEX OF COLUMNS

The everyday columns:

The holiday columns:

ABOUT THE AUTHOR

Marketta Gregory is a former religion reporter who now shares her own journey of faith with readers of her newspaper column and blog. She lives in Rochester, NY, with her husband, three sons and a very vocal Pomeranian. Visit www.SimplyFaithful.com to learn more.

61745471R00072

Made in the USA
Lexington, KY
19 March 2017